# What the FICO!

### "12 STEPS TO REPAIRING YOUR CREDIT."

## By

# Ash'Cash

**For years Ash'Cash has helped many people fix their credit! Now get the tools to fix yours too!**

# Dedication

This book is dedicated to the 44 million Americans who suffer from bad credit. Today is the beginning of your brand-new life.

# Table of Contents

# Acknowledgments

To my wife, Amina, my daughter, TJ, Sister Roz, and Mah Duke, thank you for being such a big part of my growth as a man. Without you, I would not be the person I am today.

To my team and business partners, thank you for your dedication and for helping me spread the message of fiscal responsibility far and wide. I truly appreciate all you do!

And to all my extended family and friends, those who have supported all of my endeavors, attended my workshops, and supported the Daily Word. Thanks for being an important part of my vision. Without you, I could not maximize my full potential.

**One love,**

*Ash' Cash*

Ash' Cash

# Introduction

Hi—Hello—Hola—Bonjour—Aloha—Salaam Alaikum—Shalom—Namaste—Yow Wah Gwaan—and Xin Chào!

Now that we've gotten all the pleasantries out of the way, let me get straight to the point. As the subtitle reads, this book is *12 Steps to Repairing Your Credit*. It is intended to help those who are having credit issues to rebuild good credit and restart on the journey toward the American dream and financial freedom. So many of us continue to fall into debt and not only are we finding it hard to make ends meet, but we are also having issues meeting our obligations.

Missing payments, defaults, repossessions, foreclosures, and bankruptcies do extreme damage to our credit and hinder our ability to get back on our feet. Bad credit can mean increased interest rates, decreased credit limits, or even cancelled credit privileges.

No matter what the reason for your credit decline, this book will give you step-by-step instructions on how to go from bad to good credit in a short time and with minimal cost.

Simply put, *What the FICO!* is a simple guide to repairing your credit. If you follow these simple steps (notice how many times I say "simple"), you are going to get your credit and finances back in order. This book is mainly for those who have tried to learn the credit game and have done so unsuccessfully. It can also be used by those just starting out, in order to get a better understanding of how to build a good credit history.

So why am I writing this book? As a speaker, author, and financial literacy advocate, I am part of a movement that is encouraging individuals

# Introduction

to be socially and financially responsible. With my words of inspiration about finance and lifestyle changes reaching millions of people daily, I challenge my readers to never quit and to be the best they can be. This book is part of that movement.

My main objective is to change the way you look at credit. I will give you some facts about credit and how it affects your personal life, I will share your rights as a consumer and how to protect them, and finally, I will give you 12 steps to getting your credit back on track.

This isn't a book that will take you weeks to finish. It is meant to be a quick read that you can finish in one or two days. I jump right in and give you actionable items that you can implement immediately, but I cannot stress enough that you must read it more than once to get a good grasp on how to change your financial life.

I must inform you though, that credit can be a gift or a curse! If you use it the right way, you will set your financial life on the right track and reap many benefits. If you use it the wrong way, it will wind up costing you more than you can ever imagine. Know and understand that credit is a tool. Use the tool correctly and build great things, but use it incorrectly and you will seriously hurt yourself.

When it comes to fixing your credit, there are many choices. In order to fix your credit effectively, it takes some time and patience. But if you are willing to do the work, you can go from bad to good, and even great! Some companies and programs charge thousands of dollars to do what you can do yourself. Again, it's all about the time you are willing to invest. Even more so, you have to beware of individuals and companies promising to work miracles with your credit and guarantee you things that sound too good to be true. We'll discuss it in detail later, but your score is calculated by many factors so there is NO quick fix to your credit. If someone guarantees immediate improvement on your score, then know that it is probably a scam designed to rip off vulnerable people. Many fall victim to these schemes because of desperation, but no matter how persuasive and attractive these services may seem, make sure you don't fall for them.

The only exception to the "NO quick fix" rule is Rapid Re-Score. Rapid Re-Score is a legitimate service that can help turn your credit around rather quickly. It requires a lot of money upfront and is only effective if you see obvious errors on your report. If using the Rapid Re-Score procedure, it is your responsibility to prove to the credit bureaus that they have made a mistake. You have to provide specific documents to prove it or they will deny your claim. Rapid Re-Score also requires you to pay off your credit cards in order to lower your usage and debt ratio, which accounts for 30% of your score. Simply put, this procedure helps delete mistakes and/or reports the change in your debt ratio and allows this change to take effect faster. (It will take between five and seven business days instead of the normal 30 to 60 days.) Again, it is expensive and also a short-term solution. If you do not learn how to properly maintain your credit and finances, you will find yourself back in the same rut quicker than it took you to get out.

I can't stress enough how much you DON'T need those expensive credit repair procedures. Once you fully understand how the credit game works, you will be better equipped to fix your credit issues. If, after reading this book, you still need some assistance, my suggestion would be to contact many of the FREE credit counseling services available. I provide a list of resources at the end of this book. You can also send me questions to: Questions@AskAshCash.com

Before we get started, I will give you a brief introduction about who I am and why I am qualified to teach you about fixing your credit. I am a motivational speaker, business consultant, author, and financial literacy educator. I travel the world helping everyday people get their life back in order, whether it's financially or by providing motivation through life lessons. I've been in banking for more than ten years. I ran and managed branches for some of the largest financial institutions in the world, controlling over $400 million dollars in deposits throughout my career. During my tenure in banking, I have helped countless people get their finances back in order: credit, home ownership, retirement, banking, and investments…and I still do to this day. I am also a Certified FICO Professional (FICO PRO), which is a national designation recognizing individuals who have a strong understanding of FICO® scores and how the FICO® score impacts the lender and the consumer.

Besides my professional experience, I personally struggled with credit early on. My story—and I'll make it brief—is that at eighteen years old and still living with my mother in a small two-bedroom apartment, I decided to use credit to be flashy and show off. I caused my credit score and ability to obtain credit to diminish. I bought a forty-inch TV, a DVD player with surround sound system (back when DVD players were new and expensive). Let's just say, I used this setup to entertain my friends. This irresponsibility would cost me dearly.

By twenty-one, my credit was shot. So much so that I couldn't even get approved for a department store credit card! My first car had to be leased in my girlfriend's name—who is now my wife, by the way. When it was time to get an apartment, we had to leave my name off of the application so we wouldn't get declined. In the same breath, I am the same guy who was able to fix my credit and become a homeowner by the age of 25—using what I'm about to teach you. My credit rating improved so much that I was able to finance my own car, get a major credit card with a high limit, and begin receiving daily credit offers. My goal is to teach you these methods so you too can get on the road of credit recovery.

One more thing.... Please keep an open mind! If you ever read any of my articles or books, you will notice that my goal is always to change your paradigm. Paradigm [par-uh-dahym, -dim], as defined by Webster's dictionary, is a set of assumptions, concepts, values, and practices that constitute a way of viewing reality for the community that shares them. Simply put, a paradigm is your belief system. In my best-selling book *Mind Right, Money Right: 10 Laws of Financial Freedom,* I talk about "See more, Be more™." It is the concept of "the more you experience, the more you will become." Your belief system is the way it is because you have not been exposed to anything different. My goal is to change that. This is why it is imperative to keep an open mind.

Some people growing up in an environment without proper financial education have the belief system of "money is difficult to get, money doesn't grow on trees, money is the root of all evil," and so on and so forth. These types of sayings come from having a lack mentality and will keep you down! Understand and believe that money comes easily and effortlessly, and this belief coupled with responsible action will become your reality. The following Affirmations are worth saying aloud every morning when you wake up and every night before you go to sleep:

- *I deserve to live the life of my dreams and I am open to receiving more money.*
- *My finances are getting better and better every day.*
- *I always have more than enough money to meet all of my needs.*
- *Unexpected money simply falls into my lap.*
- *I attract only lucrative, enjoyable, and beneficial circumstances.*
- *I receive money just by thinking luxuriously.*
- *I will always have more than enough money.*
- *When I open my mailbox, there is always a check for me.*
- *My wallet is bulging with money.*

By repeating these Affirmations daily begins the process of attracting more money into your life and changing your mindset about how you view the dollar. Whether you are a skeptic or not, it is imperative to try this for at least thirty days. If you do not see a change in your financial situation, then you have the right to be a skeptic. But before you've tried for thirty days, what do you have to lose?

**Disclaimer:** *Don't let your skepticism hinder you from giving it a real shot! Your reality is whatever you say it is, so if you go into any situation thinking that it will not work, then that is exactly what you will get. Keep this in mind as you begin the exercise above. Henry Ford once said, "There are those who think they can and those who think they can't, they are both right."*

## Let's get started!!

> **NOTE** Before we begin we will test your knowledge, and see what you already know about credit. At the end of each chapter you will be asked to reflect on what you just learned and be provided space to take notes

# Knowledge Test

**What is a credit score?**

_____

_____

**What are credit ratings?**

_____

_____

**What are your current credit scores?**

_____

_____

_____

**Who are the three credit score providers?**

_____

_____

_____

**What factors influence your credit score?**

_____

_____

_____

## What the FICO!

How does your credit score affect you?

_____

_____

_____


What is a "good" credit score?

_____

_____


How do you improve your credit score?

_____

_____

_____

# NOTES

_____

_____

_____

_____

_____

_____

_____

_____

_____

_____

_____

_____

_____

_____

_____

_____

_____

_____

_____

_____

# PART I

# The History of Credit and FICO Scores

The concept of credit that is "buy now, pay later" has been around for many, many years. In fact, some believe credit goes back more than three thousand years and started with the Egyptians and Babylonians. So you can imagine that credit, as we know it today, has had many evolutions. Believe it or not, not too long ago credit information was gathered by the welcome wagon representative, who would judge you based on things like the quality of your home, your furniture, opinion of your character, etc. (Welcome wagon representatives were commercial greeters who would knock on a new neighbor's door to welcome them to the neighborhood.) Back then, if you applied for a loan, the lending decisions were made based on what was on your report, which was someone's flawed opinion, and on how the underwriter at the bank felt about you. Yup, their intuitive hunch! (Another flawed opinion.) If you didn't "look right" or if you were from some minority group or lived in the wrong neighborhood, then your chances of getting credit was slim to none. Around the late 1960s, as credit became more popular, it was impossible for banks to personally interview all applicants or rely solely on the credit reports it was using. At the same time, congress had begun investigating discrimination cases that included housing loans and the practices of collection agents. Because of this, we saw the birth of three federal regulations that would forever impact the credit game. In 1971, we were introduced to the Fair Credit Reporting Act (FCRA), which tried to make sure that your credit report was accurate, fair, and private. In 1975, we were introduced to the Fair Credit Billing Act (FCBA), which tried to protect consumers from unfair billing practices and to give us (consumers) a way to address billing errors in our revolving credit accounts. And, lastly, in 1977, we were introduce to the Fair Debt Collection Practices Act (FDCPA), which tried to eliminate abusive practices by debt collectors and aimed to make sure that what was on your credit report was correct. These three regulations forced the credit reporting agencies to act in a more fair, respectable, and responsible manner. But, of course, there were loopholes.

As the information in a person's credit report became more standardized, credit providers began to rely on them more than on the gut feeling of the underwriter. Lenders started to create their own automated risk-scoring systems, but because the results were inconsistent and inaccurate they continued to look for a system that was more reliable.

Enter Bill Fair and Earl Isaac, the founders of the Fair Isaac Company, which is better known as FICO. In 1956, they started FICO as a way to develop and market their credit scoring concept. In the early years, FICO marketed their scoring system to financial service companies that were trying to find a faster and more accurate way to make credit decisions.

The breakthrough came during the late 80s as computer software automation became popular with many businesses. In 1989, FICO introduced an automated credit scoring system that was marketed as "the impartial, consistent way to evaluate credit applications, taking the prejudice and instinct out of the equation." In laymen's terms this was the most accurate, consistent, and fair way to judge someone's creditworthiness. Given that lenders were being put under pressure by congress to get rid of discriminatory lending practices, FICO seemed to be the answer to their problems and the system was quickly embraced by credit card companies and other credit issuers. This was the beginning of FICO's reign as the premier and universally accepted credit scoring system. Then, in 1995, the deal was sealed when top mortgage issuers Fannie Mae and Freddie Mac stipulated that mortgage lenders incorporate FICO Score in their approval process. This is why today the FICO Score is THE most important score as it relates to your credit.

FICO isn't the only game in town though. In fact, on the market there are hundreds of other scores sold by the credit bureaus to lenders, insurance companies, credit card companies, landlords, finance companies, telephone companies, and any other entity that needs your information for sales or marketing purposes. There are scores that tell lenders who might be more likely to default on an existing mortgage, who should be offered lower interest rates, or who should have higher limits on their credit card. There are even global scores used by large corporations conducting business internationally.

In 2006, Vantage Score was created in collaboration with the three big credit bureaus—TransUnion, Equifax, and Experian—in a concerted effort to overtake FICO's lead in the market. Vantage Score became a new generic, but exclusive, credit score model marketed as a more "consistent interpretation" and "accurate score" than FICO. FICO responded to its competition in 2009 by creating the FICO® 8 Score, which touts that its new formula will significantly enhance the score's ability to predict consumer credit risk. (We'll discuss more about this later.)

Despite all of the competition and for now, the original FICO Score—and not the FICO® 8—continues to be the clear leader and the score that matters most to your credit repair efforts. It is a fact that most lenders, with a few exceptions, use FICO in making their credit decisions. (Some banks still do manual underwriting and most employ an internal risk calculation of which FICO is only a portion.) As we continue on this journey toward repairing your credit, we will concentrate on how to control your FICO Score and make it work in your favor.

## FICO Score Tidbits

- FICO scores range from 300 to 850 and anything above 750 is excellent
- Scores are damaged by the most recently reported derogatory information
- Derogatory information reported earlier than two years prior does not highly impact your score
- FICO has 88 Negative Rating Factors and only six Positive Rating Factors
- FICO measures whether a person is moving toward or away from Bankruptcy
- There are only five basic scoring factors that you can control

**NOTE** When we refer to credit bureaus we often only talk about the Big Three—Transunion, Equifax, Experian. But it is important to know that there are other reporting agencies besides these three, but most purchase their information from the Big Three. So if you can repair your credit with the Big Three, you basically repair it with everyone. (I know I said Big Three a lot. But, hey, you get my gist!)

## Take Control of Your Credit or Your Credit Will Control You

I often hear people boast about how they don't need or use credit or, even worse, that they don't care if their credit gets "messed up." Contrary to popular belief, you do NEED credit because it controls our lives in many ways.... It controls whether we can get loans, rent an apartment, buy a home, drive that dream car, or open a bank account. It can stop you from getting a job or even that well deserved promotion.

We all know that sometimes life can hit you in the head with a brick. When that happens, some sacrifices have to be made which can include temporarily not paying back some of your creditors, but in the same breathe we must also understand that the decisions we make today can affect our lives for many years to come.

Good credit or bad credit are not these mysterious things that just happen to us by chance. Credit is something that we control and, if we understand the rules of the game and practice how we play it, we can use credit in our favor to live out our dreams.

That's why it is imperative that we always stay in the know. It is irresponsible to not know what is on our credit report and it is also irresponsible for us to not be proactive in making sure we maintain a good score. Ignorance is no excuse and Hope is not a plan! Be diligent to make sure that nothing catches you by surprise.

Your credit is yours and yours alone! This may sound harsh, but no one cares about your personal problems. At the end of the day your creditors are in business and they want to get paid! Even the credit bureaus are in it for the money. In fact, credit card debt is a $2 trillion industry that relies on the sharing of your valuable information to make big profits. As stated earlier, one source of income for the credit bureaus is to compile information about your consumer credit history and sell it to potential creditors, landlords, insurers, employers, and any willing buyer who wants to use it to send you offers. But did you know that solicitors also target individuals with low scores based on FICO because of the higher rates and fees they know they can charge? Most people believe that low scores are associated with low incomes, but those with higher income also suffer from low scores. And, given the state of the current economy, many people who never fell into this category before, are finding themselves stuck with no choices. I use the term "stuck with no choices" lightly because you always have choices. The consequences of your choices matters most and whether you are willing to pay the cost. Below are some interesting facts about credit and how it controls our lives.

# Credit Facts

- Americans are big spenders with a reported savings rate of only 3.7% as of 2012 and a total credit debt of $674 billion
- Approx 83% of divorces are due to financial problems
- Bankruptcy relief is now more difficult to file due to the new "means test"
- Minimum monthly payments for credit cards increased from 2% to 4% causing already strapped consumers financial hardship
- Any—and all—of your creditors can cancel your credit cards or increase your interest rates if you are ever late on any of your other accounts

# Credit Rating:

750+      Excellent A++
680 – 750      **Very Good A+**
620 – 680      **Good A**
580 – 680      **Above Satisfactory B**
550 – 580      **Satisfactory B-**
480 – 550      **Below Satisfactory**

# Knowledge Test

What is a FICO score?

_____

_____


Why is your credit so important?

_____

_____

_____

_____


What are the three laws that were created to protect you and your credit?

_____

_____

_____


FICO scores range from _____ to _____ and anything above _____ is excellent

How were credit decisions made in the past?

_____

_____

_____

How did FICO become so popular?

_____

_____

_____

What is a Vantage Score and why was it created?

_____

_____

What is the purpose of FICO® 8?

_____

_____

_____

# NOTES

# PART II

# How Your Credit Score Is Calculated

So the million-dollar question remains, how is your credit score calculated? Well, first you must know what exactly is in your credit report.

## What Is in Your Credit Report?

**Information that identifies you:** Your name, social security number, address, date of birth, and the name of your employer. Most of this information is supplied by you when you fill out a credit applications.

**Trade lines:** A history of your current credit obligations, which includes all of your credit cards and other accounts, the date that you opened them, your credit limit, high balance—the highest amount you have owed on the account to-date, current balance, payment history, etc.

**Credit inquiries:** Voluntary and involuntary inquiries, including account review inquiries from current lenders, hard inquiries for new loans or credit applications, and promotional inquiries for credit card companies and other solicitation offers.

**Public records:** Any bankruptcies, foreclosures, wage garnishments, liens and judgments.

**Collection accounts:** Your delinquent accounts that have been placed in a collection status by a creditor or collection agency. Delinquent accounts—for anything from a phone bill to a credit card or a medical bill—are payments that are several months late.

# Items Not Included in Your Credit Score

Although this information may appear on your credit report, it is not taken into consideration for your credit score:

- **Age**
- **Race, color, religion, nationality, sex, or marital status**
- **Occupation, salary, employer, length of time employed**
- **Where you live**
- **Interest rates charged to you on credit cards or other accounts**
- **Any item reported as child support or rental history**
- Certain types of inquiries, such as consumer-initiated inquiries or promotional inquiries

# What Goes Into Calculating My Credit Score?

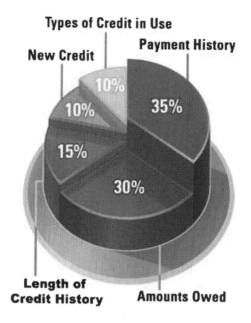

**Types of Credit in Use** — 10%

**New Credit** — 10%

**Payment History** — 35%

**Length of Credit History** — 15%

**Amounts Owed** — 30%

## Payment History (35% of your score)

- Current payment record for car loans, mortgages, retail accounts, installment loans, credit cards, and others on paid as agreed accounts
- Public records—bankruptcies, foreclosures, wage garnishments, liens and judgments
- Severity of delinquency—length of time past due
- Amount past due on accounts or collections
- Recent delinquency or collection
- Number of past due or derogatory accounts

# Payment History Tips

- Make sure you pay your bills on time because the newest late payments and collection accounts have the largest impact on the score.
- If you are past due for any reason, get current NOW! The longer you stay current and pay your bills on time, the higher your credit score will be.
- Don't be quick to close accounts. Doing so may result in losing valuable credit score points associated with that account.

# Amounts Owed (30% of your score)

- Amounts owed on revolving accounts
- Total amount owed on all accounts
- Number of accounts with balances
- Proportion of balance to credit limits on revolving accounts
- Proportion of balance still owing on installment accounts

# Amounts Owed Tips

- Keep your balances low on credit cards and other revolving accounts. A general rule of thumb is to keep your balances below 30% of the credit limit or high balance lines. For example, you should not spend more than $300 for every $1,000 you have in available credit.
- Pay off your debt instead of just moving it around. One of the most effective ways to improve your credit score is to pay down the balances on your credit cards or other revolving accounts. Owing the same amount but having fewer opened accounts may lower your score because it's increasing your usage ratio. Keep as many of your accounts below 30% of the credit limits or high balance as you can.

- Don't open new accounts to increase your available credit. This can actually backfire and lower your score.

# Length of Credit History (15% of your score)

- Age of accounts
- Number of recently opened accounts
- Time since account activity
- Proportion of new credit vs. established credit
- Re-establishment of new credit following adverse payment problems

# Length of Credit History Tips

- If you're just establishing your credit history, stay away from trying to open new accounts too soon. New accounts may bring down your score temporarily, especially if you're just starting out. Rapid account buildup can be seen as a risk to potential creditors.
- If you have past payment history problems reestablish yourself as soon as you can. Opening new accounts that you can afford to pay off on time will increase your credit score in the long term.
- Try not to open too many accounts with creditors who are known to lend to consumers with less than perfect credit history. Doing so may hinder your ability to obtain additional credit from more traditional lenders.

# Types of Credit Used (10% of your score)

The number of various types of accounts, for example, credit cards, retail accounts, installment loans, mortgages, and consumer finance accounts. This is usually called your credit mix.

# Types of Credit Tips

Only apply and open accounts as you need them; don't just do it to have them available. A good credit mix is having three open and active revolving accounts, one to two installment accounts, and one mortgage.

# New Credit / Inquiries (10% of your score)

- Number of recently opened accounts
- Number of recent inquiries
- Time since inquiry
- Time since account opening

# Types of Inquiries Explained

### Credit Inquiries

A credit inquiry appears on your report if a credit report is pulled while you are obtaining new credit or when your current lenders request it.

*Hard Inquiries*

When you apply for a mortgage, auto loan, credit card, or other type of account, you authorize the lender to obtain a copy of your credit report. These types of credit inquiries appear on your credit report and will impact your credit score by at least two points per inquiry. Stay away from applying for a lot of credit at once or jumping from lender to lender to see who will approve you. The only exception to this rule is if you are shopping for a mortgage or car. FICO gives you a 14-day, 30-day, or 45-day window to shop for and apply for credit when it's for a mortgage or car purchase, so it will count the multiple inquiries as only one.

*Account Review Inquiries and Consumer-Based Inquiries*

These types of inquiries do not affect your credit score. When you choose to pull your own credit report, it is considered a consumer-based inquiry and will not affect your credit score. (This is why it baffles me that more people are not more conscious about where they stand with their credit, but I digress.) Many creditors or collection agencies have the ability to pull your credit report to review account activity; some use it to extend more credit, some use it to take credit away. When applying for a job, credit reports pulled by a prospective employer will not affect your score either.

*Promotional Inquiries*

In many cases, a company will pull your credit report to send you pre-approved credit offers or other promotional offerings. These inquiries do not affect your credit score. You can opt-out to stop them from doing so, simply call 888-867-8688.

# Length of Time the Following Stay on Your Credit Report?

- **Bankruptcies 7, 11, or 13 = 10 Years**
- **Public Record = 10 Years**
- **Collections = 7 Years**
- **Inquiries = 2 Years**

## *FICO® 8 Score*

As previously stated, the FICO® 8 Score was created in 2009 as an enhancement to the current FICO scoring system and is said to significantly enhance the score's ability to predict how risky a consumer would be with credit. Only a handful of creditors has adopted this system, and most still use the original FICO Score. It is my prediction that, at some point, many creditors will begin to use FICO® 8. The good news is that the actions needed to maintain a good FICO® 8 Score are not too different than what it takes to maintain a good score with the current system. Paying your bills on time, keeping credit card balances low, and opening new credit accounts only when you need them are surefire ways to keep your credit rating high no matter what formula or system is used.

In an effort to keep you in the know, the following are the things that changed the most in creating the FICO® 8 Score.

### High credit card usage

FICO® 8 is more sensitive to highly utilized credit cards. So if your credit report shows a high balance close to the card's limit, your score will likely lose more points than it would have previously, so make sure you keep your monthly credit card balance low as much as possible.

### Isolated late payments

If one of your creditors reports to the credit bureau that you were at least 30 days late with your payment, your FICO® 8 score will likely lose points. If the late payment is an isolated event and your other accounts are in good standing, the FICO® 8 score is more forgiving compared with scores from previous FICO formulas. However, if your credit report shows numerous late payments, the opposite is true and your FICO® 8 Score will likely lose more points.

### Authorized users of credit card

Every generation of the FICO Score formulas has included authorized user credit card accounts when calculating a person's score. FICO® 8 continues that policy. This can help people benefit from credit accounts that they share with a joint owner. It also helps lenders by providing scores that are based on a full view of the consumer's credit history. To protect lenders and honest consumers, the FICO® 8 formula substantially reduces any benefit of so-called tradeline renting, which is a credit repair practice that adds a consumer to a stranger's good credit account to dupe lenders into thinking that the consumer is creditworthy.

## Small-balance collections accounts

FICO® 8 ignores small-dollar collection accounts in which the original balance was less than $100. (That doesn't mean to forget those accounts nor does it give you a pass to act irresponsibly.)

Again I implore you to:
- Pay your bills on time
- Keep your credit card balances low
- And open new credit accounts only when you need them

# Knowledge Test

What is in your credit report?

_____

_____

_____

_____

What goes into calculating your credit score?

_____

_____

_____

_____

What are the three types of credit inquiries and which one affects your credit the most?

_____

_____

_____

(Circle One) True or False
If you check your own credit more than once a year, it will negatively affect your score.

## What the FICO!

How long does bankruptcies, public records, collections, and inquiries stay on your credit report?

_____

_____

_____


What are three ways to manage your credit effectively?

_____

_____

_____

_____

# NOTES

_____

_____

_____

_____

_____

_____

_____

_____

_____

_____

_____

_____

_____

_____

_____

_____

_____

_____

_____

_____

_____

_____

## PART III

# Your Rights as a Consumer

---

So, now for the good stuff and the bulk of what's going to help you get from bad to good (or even great) credit: **YOUR RIGHTS AS A CONSUMER!**

As stated earlier, in **1971**, we were introduced to the **Fair Credit Reporting Act (FCRA)**, which <u>tried</u> to make sure you have a credit report that is accurate, fair, and private. In **1975,** we were introduced to the **Fair Credit Billing Act (FCBA)** and its <u>**purpose was**</u> to protect consumers from unfair billing practices and to give us (consumers) a way to address billing errors in our revolving credit accounts. And lastly, in **1977**, we were introduce to the **Fair Debt Collection Practices Act (FDCPA)**, which <u>tried</u> to eliminate abusive practices by debt collectors and <u>**aimed to**</u> ensure our credit report was correct.

Even though all of these laws are still in effect, when describing them you probably notice that I used phrases like **"tried" "aimed to"** and **"its purpose was."** This is because for the past 40 years, credit bureaus, lenders, and collection agencies have ignored most of the laws. For example, information about you **has to be accurate and**

**verified before it is entered on your credit report.** If **reasonable procedures** have not been correctly followed, then **any unverified items or inaccuracies must be removed from your credit reports** as defined in the **FCRA**. But I'm jumping ahead of myself.... Below is a more detailed explanation of the three federal laws and how they will assist you in your credit repair efforts.

# Fair Credit Reporting Act (FCRA)

The Fair Credit Reporting Act or FCRA, as we will now call it, is the biggest reason why things like race, religion, and people's opinion of you can no longer be included in your credit report or be the basis of a credit decision. It is also the reason why "you" (the consumer) can even see what is being reported on your credit file. Prior to FCRA, credit reports were NEVER disclosed to consumers. (Yup! They never told you why you were being approved or declined, they just made a decision and you had to take it or leave it.) This is pivotal, because what FCRA has essentially done is guaranteed that everyone is treated consistently and fairly when it comes to obtaining credit.

FCRA also makes sure that you can get your consumer credit reports at a reasonable price (or for free under certain circumstances). It regulates who has permission to view your consumer report and it puts a maximum limit on how long items can remain on your report—two years on inquiries, seven years for most negative items, and 10 years on bankruptcy and public records.

An important thing to keep in mind is that these are only MAXIMUM limits. FCRA does not say that there's a MINIMUM time something must remain on your credit report. Basically, FCRA protects you against something remaining on your report forever, but has no requirement that says that items have to be on there for a minimum length. With that being said, it's worth remembering that credit reports are not official government documents. Credit bureaus are not officially sanctioned agencies, but FOR-PROFIT businesses and, just like any other for-profit business, the right price can get anything done (wink, wink).

# How Can FCRA Assist in Credit Repair Efforts?

Anytime you dispute an item on your credit report, the credit bureau that you are disputing it with—remember we are only concentrating on the Big Three—must note within your file that the item is being disputed. This MUST begin an investigation that MUST be completed within a REASONABLE amount of time, which the industry standard says is 30 days. The credit bureau MUST then inform you of what action was taken: either it's verified (the item remains as is), modified (certain things in the item have been revised), deleted (the item is removed from your file), or deemed "frivolous" (a provision that allows the credit bureau to basically say you're not being serious). Based on their decision you then have the right to exercise other options. (We'll discuss other options later.)

# Fair Debt Collection Practices Act (FDCPA)

I can't begin to tell you the things that collection agencies would do in an attempt to collect debt! If you've ever fallen behind on a bill and had a collection agency contact you, I'm sure you have your own war stories. To be fair, it's not all of them, but for the most, part collection agencies were rude, forceful, demeaning, and manipulative! (Some still are.) Some debt collectors were so creative and crafty (cunning is what I mean to say, but I'm trying to be nice) that they would sometimes disguise themselves as old friends or, oppositely, they would berate you and then threaten you with wage garnishment or jail. Do you believe that some even pretended to be official government agencies acting on behalf of your creditors? Yup! Those low down dirty bast.... (Sorry, you can tell I've been a victim.)

The Fair Debt Collection Practices Act or FDCPA was enacted to protect you from this abusive behavior. FDCPA was also created to stop collectors from harassing you day and night, speaking with your neighbors, boss, mother, brother, cousin, or anyone else about your personal matter. I've even heard stories of collectors contacting your Facebook friends and following you on Twitter. Ha! But wait. Wasn't FDCPA enacted in 1977? And aren't Facebook and Twitter relatively new? Yup. And unfortunately, even though these laws are in effect, because we don't know any better too many of us allow this stuff to go on! Being late on bills or not being able to meet certain obligations does not make you a criminal so you should not be treated as one.

One good thing is that FDCPA allows you to document any abuses (as stated above) and there are stiff penalties and consequences for those collection agencies that think they're above the law. Another good—or great—thing is that the FDCPA allows you to demand proof that a collector even owns an alleged debt. Cha-Ching!!!!

In a nutshell:
- Collection agencies can ONLY contact you via telephone between the hours of 8:00 a.m. and 9:00 p.m. (local time).
- If you submit a written request to ask a collection agency to stop contacting you, they MUST comply (unless they are taking you to court).
- Collection agencies CANNOT call you repeatedly or engage anyone in your household—including you—on a phone conversation with the intention to annoy, abuse, or harass.
- If you advise a collection agency that it is unacceptable or prohibited by your employer, collection agencies CANNOT communicate with you at your place of employment.
- Collection agencies CANNOT contact you if they know you are being represented by legal counsel.
- If you ask the collection agency via a written request to validate your debt (prove they have the right to collect), they MUST stop communication with you until they provide you with this validation or the original creditor's name and address.
- Collection agencies CANNOT misrepresent themselves or deceive you into paying your debt. For example, saying that they are an attorney or law enforcement officer.

- Collection agencies CANNOT publish your name or address on any so-called "bad debt" list.
- Collection agencies CANNOT ask you to pay any unjustified amount of money that was not covered in the original contract or that is not allowed by law.
- Collection agencies CANNOT threaten you with arrest or legal action that is either not permitted or that they have no real intention of pursuing.
- Collection agency reps CANNOT use profanity or abusive language while talking to you in reference to your debt.
- Collection agencies CANNOT communicate with any third parties or reveal any specific information about your debt (other than to your spouse or attorney).
- Collection agencies CANNOT report false information on your credit report or threat to do so while trying to collect a debt.

# How Can FDCPA Assist in Your Credit Repair Efforts?

It is important to note that collection agencies are a for-profit business making money from collecting debt. In fact, most of your original creditors will attempt to collect the money you owe using their internal collectors, but if they are unsuccessful they will sell your debt to a collection agency for pennies on the dollar. For example, if you have an account with Macy's and owe them...let's say...$1,000. Macy's will try their best to collect what you owe, but after so many failed attempts they will sell your $1,000 debt to ABC collection agency for $200 and will write off the $800 difference (acknowledge the debt as a loss). This is why collection agencies are always quick to settle with you; they know that even if you give them $500 of the $1000 debt, they still win because they bought your debt for $200. Sometimes if one collection agency isn't successful in collecting the debt they will sell it to another then another then another! That's why you'll notice different companies trying to collect the same debt—and there lies your power.

FDCPA specifically details your right to request further information regarding any alleged debt. This is what the industry calls debt validation and it is incredibly POWERFUL in your credit repair efforts! Understand that you have the right to challenge the accuracy of any debt. Once challenged, the debt collection agencies MUST respond in a certain way or else they MUST stop contacting you and REMOVE any related information to that debt from your credit report. We'll discuss validation in more detail later, but it can become the central tool you use to get negative items removed from your credit report (and even the ones that are valid but you didn't hear that from me).

# Fair Credit Billing Act (FCBA)

Just like how FDCPA protects you from collection agencies, the Fair Credit Billing Act or FCBA protects you from your original creditors. It simply requires that your creditors bill you correctly and completely and absolves you of ANY responsibility in the event an error was made. The following are examples of billing errors under the FCBA:

- Charges that you DID NOT make
- Charges that are for the WRONG amount
- Charges for goods or services that you DID NOT receive
- Charges for goods NOT delivered as agreed
- Charges for goods that were DAMAGED on delivery
- FAILURE to properly reflect payments or credits to an account
- Calculation ERRORS
- Charges that you want CLARIFICATION for or that you request PROOF of
- Statements mailed to the WRONG address

# How Can FCBA Assist in Your Credit Repair Efforts?

The Federal Trade Commission is the governing body that enforces the FCBA and, while it prohibits all that I listed above, the most helpful part related to your credit repair efforts is the fact that the commission mandates your original creditors to ASSUME RESPONSIBILITY for INCORRECT REPORTING and for the ILLEGAL activities of affiliated third-party debt collectors. In plain English, your original creditors are required to take responsibility for the shady things done by the debt collectors they sold your debt to! Cha-ching! Cha-ching!!!

# Your Consumer Rights Are Just The Beginning!

*Knowing your rights and using them in your favor are a big part of getting your credit back on track. But as you will see in the 12 steps, that is just the beginning. Nothing will ever replace being responsible. Things will always happen in life that seem beyond our control, but proper preparation and responsible decision making will always keep you on the straight and narrow.*

Without any further ado—12 STEPS TO REPAIRING YOUR CREDIT!

# Knowledge Test

What does FCRA stand for and how does it protect you?

_____

_____

_____

(Circle One) True or False
FCRA puts a maximum limit on how long items can remain on your credit report but does not mandate a minimum.

Name three things that collection agencies CANNOT do as per FDCPA?

_____

_____

_____

What is the most powerful tool that FDCPA provides you in your credit repair efforts?

_____

_____

_____

# What the FICO!

How does the Fair Credit Billing Act protect You?

_____

_____

_____

Who is the governing body that enforces FCBA?

_____

_____

_____

# NOTES

_____

_____

_____

_____

_____

_____

_____

_____

_____

_____

_____

_____

_____

_____

_____

_____

_____

_____

_____

_____

_____

_____

_____

_____

_____

# PART IV

# 12 Steps to Repairing Your Credit

---

So now that you understand how FICO works, I won't waste any more time. The following are 12 steps that you should implement immediately in order to repair your credit and get back on the road to financial freedom.

Before you begin, go to **www.AnnualCreditReport.com** to order a FREE copy of your credit report from the Big Three credit bureaus. AnnualCreditReport.com is the ONLY official site that gives you your credit report for FREE. (The site is sponsored by the Big Three because they are required by LAW to give you one free report each year.) Don't get confused by all of the other credit report sites that promote giving you a FREE report/score or have FREE in their name; most actually charge you a fee after an initial trial period.

**NOTE**

www.AnnualCreditReport.com ONLY offers your credit report for FREE, if you want to get your score you will have to pay to obtain it. EACH of the three credit bureaus all have their own website that offer access to your score for a nominal fee

# Step 1 – Remove mistakes from your credit report:

The most important thing to do with your credit reports is to review them for accuracy. It is tough enough paying for your own mistakes, but having to pay for someone else's is absolutely unacceptable. Remember, your rights as a consumer state that information about you has to be accurate and verified before it is entered on your credit reports. If reasonable procedures have not been correctly followed, then any unverified items or inaccuracies and/or erroneous or obsolete information MUST be removed from your credit reports as defined in FCRA.

**Inaccurate information** is any information that cannot be verified by the credit bureau and/or the creditor.

**Erroneous information** is any information entered onto your credit reports due to human error (such as, a data entry error), social security number mismatch error, mixed file error, similar names error, reasonable procedures were not followed when the information was entered on your credit report, or any other related error(s). This happens more often than you think. These are the reasons why it's important to check your report often!

**Obsolete information** is any information that is beyond the industry standard of seven years or ten years for bankruptcy and public records.

Once you identify any inaccurate, erroneous, or obsolete information on your credit report, you must contact—in writing—the credit bureau(s)
IMMEDIATELY!

> **NOTE** Not all creditors or collection agencies report to all three bureaus, so it is possible that information contained within one may not be on the others. That's why it is imperative that you check all three.

# 12 Steps to Repairing Your Credit

Steps to resolve errors:

1. Write a letter to the credit bureaus stating what information you believe is inaccurate. Once you do so, they MUST investigate the item(s) within 30 days, unless they consider your dispute frivolous.

2. Include copies—not originals—of any documents to support your claim. Also, include your complete name, address, and social security number.

3. Clearly identify each item in your report that you are disputing, state the facts, explain why you are disputing the information, then request a deletion or correction. You should enclose a copy of your credit report with the questionable items circled or clearly marked.

4. Send your letter by certified mail—return receipt requested—so that you can document that the credit bureau(s) received all of your correspondence. Keep copies of your dispute letter and enclosures.

**NOTE** NEVER USE THE ELECTRONIC INTERNET DISPUTE OPTION ON THE CREDIT BUREAUS WEBSITE! By doing so, you give up many of your rights. In order to use the credit bureau's service, you are required to agree to its terms and conditions that if a disputed item is returned "verified," you have no right to re-dispute the item. You'll see in the next step why this is important to reserve this right.

Also, **YOU SHOULD NEVER USE AN INTERNET TEMPLATE FOR YOUR DISPUTES.** Most of the credit bureaus use a computer system to scan any letters and, if it's an Internet template, they can deny your claim stating that your inquiry is frivolous. The best option is to use the sample letters below as a guide. But use your own words and handwrite it with black or blue ink.

# What the FICO!

Removing Mistakes Sample Letter:

Date
Your Name
Your Social Security Number
Your Address
Your City, State, Zip Code

Complaint Department
Name of Credit Bureau
Address
City, State, Zip Code

Dear Sir or Madam:

I am writing to dispute the following information in my file. The items I dispute also are encircled on the attached copy of the report I received.

This item [identify item(s) disputed by name of source, such as creditors or tax court, and identify type of item, such as credit account, judgment, etc.] is [inaccurate or incomplete] because [describe what is inaccurate or incomplete and why]. I am requesting that the item be deleted [or request another specific change] to correct the information.

Enclosed are copies of [use this sentence, if applicable, and describe any enclosed documentation, such as payment records, court documents] supporting my position. Please reinvestigate this [these] matter(s) and [delete or correct] the disputed item(s) as soon as possible.

Sincerely,

Your name

Enclosures: (List what you are enclosing)

You should also write the creditor(s) or organization(s) that provided the inaccurate, erroneous, or obsolete information, explaining to them that you are disputing the information sent to the credit bureau(s). Include copies of the documents that support your claim. Make sure you send this information to their dispute department; most have specific addresses for disputes. Also send this information via certified mail with return receipt requested.

The process of removing mistakes from your credit report can take between 30 and 90 days. If the creditor(s) or organization(s) that provided the inaccurate, erroneous, or obsolete information report the same information to the credit bureaus, a notice of your dispute MUST be included. Also request that the information provider copy you on any correspondence being sent to the bureaus.

**NOTE** In many states, once a dispute has been made you are eligible to receive a free credit report directly from the credit bureaus. This is done so you can verify the updated information. Contact the appropriate credit bureau to see if you qualify for this service. (Contact information for the credit bureaus are provided in the resources section of this book.)

# Step 2 – Remove negative items from your report—legally and permanently

This is the part of the book where many of the credit repair companies are going to cringe because I am giving away their secrets. As stated, many of them charge thousands of dollars for a service that you can pretty much do yourself, all you need is patience and follow-through. This process is simple, but I must caution you that you need to do it the right way or the credit bureaus will deny your request and call it frivolous, which is the term they often use to say that you are not being serious.

To make things clear, the credit bureaus are private, for-profit businesses. They are not a government agency and surely not a charity created for the betterment of the creditors. With that said, as for-profit, nongovernmental agencies, they are LEGALLY bound by the FCRA and MUST follow the law to protect consumers. FCRA states that they are ONLY allowed to have negative items on your credit report if they are 100% accurate and verifiable.

Dictionary.com defines accurate as "free from error or defect; consistent with a standard, rule, or model; precise; exact."

Verifiable simply means possible to verify or able to show proof of. When FCRA uses "accurate" it means that ALL information MUST be CORRECT (name, social security number, account opening date, amount owed, or account numbers).

According to Bankrate.com, roughly 70% of ALL credit report files have mistakes on them, so it is very likely that yours does too.

Credit bureaus also HAVE TO make sure that information reported on your credit report is VERIFIABLE to you upon your request (within 15 days from the date they conclude their investigation).

The credit bureaus also MUST—upon your request—provide you with the METHOD OF VERIFICATION, which includes the name, address, and phone number of the organization that provided the verification, as well as proof that they received a copy of the ORIGINAL dated contract with your SIGNATURE on it.

So here's the good news. Just like many for-profit businesses that cut corners in an attempt to save money, the credit bureaus use a standard electronic and automated dispute process, which is processed out of the country. This almost guarantees that they DO NOT have the verifiable information needed to validate your debt if you ask them. Ah-ha! This little known fact and your right to request a METHOD OF VERIFICATION PROOF is your smoking gun!

For years the credit bureaus HAVE NOT complied with the law and, because most consumers are not aware of their rights, the credit bureaus get away with it. By simply requesting a METHOD OF VERIFICATION you can force them to comply and in turn remove any unverifiable negative item from your credit report! Cha-Ching!!

By using this method, you are telling the credit bureaus that you know your rights and demand to be treated fairly. But, you also signal to them that you understand that, because they cannot verify the item, they MUST delete it or you will file a complaint with the Federal Trade Commission, which regulates the credit bureaus.

**NOTE** You can only use the METHOD OF VERICATION request after you send a letter of dispute to the credit bureaus and receive a "verified" or "new information below" response from them.

Again, I stress **NEVER USE THE ELECTRONIC INTERNET DISPUTE OPTION ON A CREDIT BUREAU'S WEBSITE!** By doing so you give up many of your rights. In fact, in order to use the credit bureau's service, you are required to agree to its terms and conditions that if a disputed item is returned "verified," you have no right to re-dispute the item.

Also remember that disputes MUST be sent via certified mail with delivery confirmation. In the event that you have to file a complaint with the FTC, you need to show them proof that the credit bureaus received your correspondence. Another little known fact is that the credit bureaus would rather delete items than waste time going back and forth with the FTC.

Steps to remove negative items:
**1) Write a letter of dispute and send it to each credit bureau. (Addresses to the credit bureaus are provided in the resources section of this book.)**
Make sure that you send the letter to ALL three credit bureaus, not just one.

**REMEMBER: NEVER USE AN INTERNET TEMPLATE TO MAKE YOUR DISPUTES.** Most of the credit bureaus use a computer system to scan letters and, if it's an Internet template, they can deny your claim and state that your inquiry is frivolous. The best option is to use the sample letter as a guide, but use your own words and handwrite it with black or blue ink.

> **NOTE** The dispute letter in the previous step (Step 1- Remove mistakes from your credit report) is to remove MISTAKES from your report. The one used in this step is slightly different because you are attempting to remove NEGATIVE items from your report and it must include verbiage about verification

## Removing Negative Items Sample Letter:

Date
Your Name
Your Social Security Number
Your Address
Your City, State, Zip Code

Complaint Department
Name of Credit Bureau
Address
City, State, Zip Code

## Re: Inaccurate information on my credit report

Dear Sir or Madam:
    I am writing to dispute the following listed accounts:
1.   ABC Creditor, Account #1234567
2.   DEF Creditor, Account #89765

Due to the inaccuracy of this information, I am requesting that you delete it from my file.

Please also provide me with the description of the procedure that you used to determine the accuracy and completeness of the above items within 15 days of you completing your investigation. Under federal law you have 30 days to complete your investigation.

Thank you in advance for your immediate attention to this matter.

Sincerely,


Your name

# What the FICO!

After you send the letter, it should take about 30 days to receive a response. If a credit bureau responds with a letter stating that the item(s) is deleted, then great! You won! If it's another decision, then proceed to #2 below.

> **NOTE** If the credit bureaus deleted some—and not all—use the next step for the ones that remain. DO NOT mention the ones that have been deleted.

2) If you receive a "verified" or "new information below" response from the credit bureaus, send a "Method of Verification" letter to them. **REMEMBER: DO NOT USE AN INTERNET TEMPLATE.** Use the below sample letter as a guide but use your own words and handwrite it with black or blue ink.

## Method of Verification Sample Letter:

Date
Your Name
Your Social Security Number
Your Address
Your City, State, Zip Code

Complaint Department
Name of Credit Bureau
Address
City, State, Zip Code

## Re: Request to provide Method of Verification

Dear Sir or Madam:
    On [Insert Original Date of Dispute], I requested an investigation of items on my report that were not reported legally, and

on [Insert Date of Response], I received a letter stating that your investigation was complete. Please explain to me how you conducted your investigation.

1. Please explain what your representatives uncovered to lead them to believe that you are reporting this item as it legally should be reported?

2. What certified documents were reviewed to conclude your investigation?

3. Please provide a complete copy of all of the information that was transmitted to the furnisher of data as part of the investigation.

4. What did it cost your company to obtain the documents needed to complete your investigation?

5. Please provide proof of your timely procurement of certified documents.

6. Did you speak directly to any agent of the company that was reporting the information to confirm the accuracy of what you are reporting?

7. If yes to number 6 above:
   a. Who did you speak to?
   b. On what date?
   c. How long was the conversation?
   d. What was their job title?
   e. What telephone number did you call?
   f. What is the name of the employee from your company who spoke directly to the above party?
   g. What is the job title of the employee of your company who spoke directly to the above party?
   h. How long has that employee been employed by your company?
   i. What formal training was provided to this employee to investigate items of this kind?
   j. Was there any e-mail or written communication between members of your company and the above party?

8. If there has been written communications, please provide copies of all correspondence, copies of any and all conclusive documentation to prove that you have, in fact, conducted a reasonable investigation of the account in question.
9. Provide the date of the commencement of delinquency.
10. Provide the SPECIFIC date reporting that these items will cease.

This inaccurate reporting has caused me major financial and emotional distress. Please reply within 15 days to the above questions or delete the items.

Sincerely,


your name


3) If the credit bureaus cannot verify the item but refuse to delete it, or they do not reply to your inquiry within a desired timeframe, then send a letter of intent to file a formal complaint to the FTC.

## Notice of Intent Sample Letter:

Date
your Name
your Social Security Number
your Address
your City, State, Zip Code

Complaint Department
Name of Credit Bureau
Address
City, State, Zip Code

## Re: Inaccurate information on my credit report

Dear Sir or Madam:

RE: Dispute Letter dated [date of initial letter], and Follow-up Letter dated [date of second letter]

NOTICE OF INTENT TO FILE FORMAL FTC COMPLAINT

This letter shall serve as formal notice of my intent to file a complaint with the Federal Trade Commission (FTC), due to your failure to respond to my two previous letters requesting a correction to my credit file.

As indicated by the enclosed copies of letters and mailing receipts, you have received from me, by registered mail, a dispute letter dated [date of initial letter], as well as a follow-up letter, dated [date of second letter].

I am sure that you are aware of the Fair Credit Reporting Act's requirement to respond to consumer's credit report disputes within 30 days, and that the FTC investigates complaints for failure to respond. I have advised you on two separate occasions, more than 75 days ago and again 40 days ago, that you are reporting inaccurate information about me. For the record and your benefit, I will restate my dispute:

Line Item: [insert name of creditor, account number or line item number]

Item Description: [this info is found on your credit report]

Requested Correction: Please delete the above item(s)

The item above is completely [insert appropriate word: inaccurate, incorrect, incomplete, erroneous, misleading, outdated] and needs to be corrected immediately. I have enclosed a copy of your organization's credit report dated [insert date of report here] and for your convenience, circled the item(s) described above.

If you do not immediately take steps to resolve this issue, I will be forced to file a formal complaint with the FTC. Furthermore, I intend to consider seeking redress in civil court to recover damages, costs, and attorney fees, should you fail to respond.

# What the FICO!

Furthermore, I expect you to supply me with a description of the procedure used to determine the accuracy and completeness of the disputed information, provide a corrected credit profile to me, a list of all creditors who have received a copy of my credit report within the last six months and the last two years for employment purposes, and the name, address, and telephone number of each credit grantor or other subscriber that received a copy of my credit profile within the last six months.

If your reinvestigation was negative, please supply the description of the procedure used to determine the accuracy and completeness of the information to my address above. If you have any questions concerning this matter I can be reached at [insert daytime phone number, including area code].

Sincerely,


Your name


Honestly, everything should be resolved after step two, but sending the intent to file a complaint letter should work. Typically credit bureaus would rather delete items than waste their time going back and forth with the FTC.

In the rare event that you send the third letter and your item is still not removed, I would suggest that you file a real complaint with the FTC and let them investigate the matter.

> **NOTE** Patience is your best friend when going through this procedure. It may at first seem tedious and time consuming, but I promise you that it is worth the effort. To see you credit score jump 80 to 100 points because of negative items being deleted is something worth waiting for.

# Step 3- Create A Budget

One of the biggest reasons many people find themselves head over heals in debt is because they DO NOT properly budget their expenses. They do a poor job planning how to allocate their funds and wind up spending money as things come up. Many of those things include impulse spending, which leaves little money for the necessities and forces them to borrow to cover the difference. Creating a budget is building your road map for success. Not only will it allow you to figure out how much money you can allocate towards the repayment of your debt, but it will also assure that you will not get back into debt going forward. The rule of thumb is that your debt repayment should not be higher than 40% of your net income, which is income after taxes and deductions. But my suggestion is that you come up with a budget that you WILL FOLLOW, then revisit it monthly to gauge your success. Based on your findings, adjust your plan (if needed) with the ultimate goal to increase your savings and reduce your debts.

*Steps to create a budget:*

## 1) Write Down Your Financial Goals

If you don't know where you're going, then any path will lead you there! It is important that you set your financial goals ahead of time so that you can track your progress along the way. Obviously, because you are reading this book, we know that one of your financial goals is to fix your credit. But after you are successful, think about building savings, buying a new home, giving to charity, or other goals. Whatever it is (or they are), make sure you write them down—both short-term and long-term goals—and review them monthly (or how many times you need) to stay motivated and focused!

## 2) Track Your Spending for a Month

When creating budgets, many people fool themselves by only including regular expenses like rent, phone, or electricity. They don't realize that it is the small, unaccounted expenses, like constantly eating out or unnecessary cab fares, that throw you off. Tracking your spending for a month will alleviate the involuntary amnesia and will help you recognize your spending habits in order to plug the leaks. No dollar should escape being accounted for. Every cent that leaves your pocket (or your debit card) should be written down in a small journal, checkbook ledger, or a sticky note. When I say EVERY CENT, I mean EVERY CENT, no matter how small!

To assure that you don't miss anything, you also need to get and keep all of your important documents together. This should include all financial statements, investments, pay stubs, dividend statements, annuities, child support, alimony, everything. Anything you pay out each month and everything you receive as income. This will help you get organized in order to create the budget accurately and truly understand your bottom line.

# Bottom Line = Income - Expenses

### 3) Decide How Your Funds Will Be Allocated

Once you know where your money is going, you can make an educated decision about how to best allocate it. Many people make the grave mistake of trying to be too conservative. They think that creating a budget is about deprivation, so they cut out all things that are fun (at least on paper) and think that they can follow this strict budget! PLEASE DO NOT do this! The number one rule when setting up your budget is to NOT cut out all the fun from your life. Your budget must be realistic. You work hard for your money, so there must be a balance between work and play! Budgets that have no allowance for entertainment are doomed to fail.

There are many different budget allocation guidelines that you can follow, but, because everyone's situation is different, I suggest you use what you are most likely to be able to stick to. Remember that your debt allocation shouldn't be more than 40% of your take-home pay and you MUST pay yourself first by putting money aside for savings and emergencies. Six to eight months of expenses saved in an account for emergencies is a good start, so make sure this is included as one of your short-term goals.

## 4) Determine the Budget Method and Tools You Will Use and Start Your Budget

Decide which budget method you will use—manual or electronic? Pencil and paper or software? Envelopes or online banking? Dry erase board or Excel worksheet? It really doesn't matter which you choose, just make sure it is user friendly. Once you decide, input/write down all the sources of income that you receive, then input/write down all of your expenses, recording everything that has to be paid each month.

Total up all of your income and expenses making sure that expenses aren't greater than income. If income is greater than expenses, congratulations you have a positive bottom line and more money to save and pay down debt. If expenses are greater than income, then your bottom line is negative and you must make adjustments IMMEDIATELY. There are only three ways that you can increase your bottom line:

1) Cut Expenses
2) Increase Income or
3) Do both!

To cut expenses, first try to minimize or limit things that are not a necessity.

## 5) Adjust Your Budget at the Beginning of Every Month, if Necessary

Even the US Constitution has amendments, so don't, for a second, think that you will just create your budget once and that will be it! Make sure you are flexible and that you are keeping your eye open for any life changes. The budget process is a lifelong process, so keep adjusting and keep living within your means.

Review your budget monthly to check your progress on some of your short- and long-term goals and make all the necessary adjustments as things change. Remember again, the goal is to get out of debt and save more. As you pay down your debt, DO NOT reestablish any bad habits that will set you back. Having extra money is not a sin…self-discipline is key! Learn to save more and control your urges.

# Sample Budget Form

**MY BUDGET SHEET**                    WEEK: _____

INCOME:                                          AMOUNT:
Allowance:                                        _____
Earnings:                                         _____
Gifts: (birthdays/holidays)                  _____
Other:                                             _____
                                   INCOME TOTAL: _____

FIXED EXPENSES:                            AMOUNT:
_____          _____
_____          _____
_____          _____
_____          _____
_____
                        FIXED EXPENSES TOTAL: _____


INCOME TOTAL - FIXED EXPENSES TOTAL=: _____


OTHER/UNEXPECTED EXPENSES:            AMOUNT:
_____          _____
_____          _____
_____          _____
_____          _____
_____          _____
_____          _____
_____          _____
_____
                        OTHER EXPENSES TOTAL: _____

# Step 4 – Negotiate with Your Creditors and Collection Agencies

At this point anything that is still on your credit report has been validated, meaning that you are fully responsible. If it is a negative item that you have already paid off, then there really isn't anything that you can do but wait it out and let it fall off of your report—seven years for negative items, 10 years for bankruptcies and public records. If you still owe money and can either pay in full or make payment arrangements, then you have true bargaining power!

As I stated previously, your creditors are in the business of making money…and for the right price and right circumstance, you can make almost anything go away! (We're still talking about credit folks! Lol!). Your creditors are not government agencies and NOWHERE in the law does it mandate that negative items HAVE TO be reported. With that said, when a creditor or collection agency reports information to the credit bureaus they are doing so voluntarily and can, theoretically, remove or modify what they are reporting to be less negative. If you can convince them to do so.

In essence, the severity of what the creditor or collection agency reports is at their discretion or if they even report to begin with. So it would be in your best interest to be proactive when dealing with your creditors and the collection agencies. When you contact them and are ready to make either a full payment or some type of payment arrangement, they will sometimes work with you or show mercy when sending information to the credit bureaus. Please be clear, this is NEVER something a creditor or collection agency would do automatically. You have to be ready to negotiate, and here's how:

## 1) Decide how much is the maximum you can pay for each debt that you are going to negotiate.

If you can pay a lump sum, then know the amount you are willing to pay. Or if you can only afford monthly payments, know that number as well. Either way you must be ready to make a payment. It is important to note that you have more negotiating power if you can settle your account by paying one lump sum, as opposed to using a payment plan.

## 2) Make the call to your creditor or collection agency inquiring about the debt.

Be very inquisitive and surprised at the amount they say you owe. Be cooperative and seem willing to right your wrongs. Don't be defensive and don't be rude, even if they are. Don't allow them to be pushy or scare you. Understand that their job is to collect the debt by any means. In essence, I am saying that you need to eat some humble pie before you make the call and don't let your ego get the best of you. Remember that your goal is to pay off the debt or set up a payment plan without it reflecting negatively on your credit report, so this isn't the time to worry about your feelings. This may require a little swallowing of your pride, but once you pull it off you'll realize that it was well worth it. One important piece to remember is that, even in being humble, you MUST remain confident at all times. The moment you seem timid or afraid is the moment that you lose some negotiating power. The key is at ALL times to remain professional and not intimidated.

## 3) Figure out what the creditor or collection agency is willing to accept as a settlement.

Asking to pay between 50 and 70 percent of what you owe is actually a reasonable offer. Again, you are more likely to get a favorable answer if you can pay it as a lump sum, but you still have a good shot if all you can afford is to set up a payment plan. I've seen people get this done is one call and others it took several rounds of negotiation. Don't fret and don't give up so easy. If your request is denied, ask to speak with a supervisor who may have more authority to get things done. Once your settlement request is granted, ask that the settlement be reported to the credit bureaus as paid in full or deleted completely from your record. (Usually, collection agencies will only agree to delete a record if the debt is paid in full, not settled, but it's worth a shot.)

## 4) Ask for any agreements in writing.

It is your job to protect your own interests, just like it is the creditor or collection agency's job to protect theirs. Do not think for a second that someone working for a creditor or collection agency will have your best interests at heart. No matter what they say, they do not care about your problems and they not care about you! They simply want to collect the money that is owed to them or the company they represent. With that said NEVER take their word for ANYTHING! Even though they usually say, "This call may be monitored or recorded for quality assurance purposes," don't take that to mean that they are bound by what they tell you. If it is said verbally, but not written down, then it did not really happen. Once you get a verbal confirmation on your agreement, send your negotiation offer in writing and map out all of the terms, or request that they do the same. Make sure you ask them to sign and date a copy of the agreement and return it to you so that you can keep it for your records. Also, make sure you understand exactly what you're committing to, if not, consult a lawyer or credit counselor.

## 5) Make your payment as agreed

Now that you have everything in writing, it is time to keep up your end of the bargain. NEVER give your bank information to your creditors or collection agencies if you can help it. I've heard horror stories of people having their bank accounts wiped out by collection agencies then going through hell trying to recover the money. When asked how you are going to pay, explain to them that you will be paying by cashier's check or money order. If they insist on a debit card payment or checking account to set up automatic drafts, then make sure you open an account specifically for that debt and only transfer money into it as needed.

> **BONUS** The above speaks specifically to items on your credit report that are already past due, but if you are having issues or foresee having issues with accounts that are current and paid as agreed, then there are many options that you can use to negotiate a more affordable term.

# What the FICO!

If you are having issues paying, make sure you contact your creditors IMMEDIATELY! Not after months of harassing calls, but as soon as you realize you won't be able to make payments. Being proactive can really work in your favor because it shows your willingness to pay your obligations and signals to your creditor that you are not a deadbeat, but are actually going through some financial problems. I've seen cases where people were able to negotiate a lower monthly payment, defer one or more payments, have late fees and penalties waived, lower their interest rate, or have their loan restructured to make paying it off more affordable.

If you are able to negotiate a better term, make sure you request that they send a letter confirming it.

# Step 5 – Pay at Least the Minimum Due on Your Credit Accounts (On Time!)

This probably goes without saying but DO NOT arrange a lowered settlement amount that you CANNOT pay. It will only reflect badly on your credit and put you deeper in a hole. Previously, you saw in the breakdown of how your FICO Score works, payment history is the number one factor in your credit score that you can control and is over one-third of your score.

Besides the fact that you have just spent your valuable time calling, mailing, and negotiating better terms, not following through will ASSURE that negative items are placed on your report and it will almost be impossible to renegotiate a second time.

This is why it is IMPERATIVE that you create your budget and follow it religiously, PRIOR to negotiating with your creditors and collection agencies. Your budget gives you a blueprint as to how much you can afford and it alleviates the possibility of not being able to follow through.

> **CAUTION** If you were not successful in negotiating a settlement or record deletion from an old collection account, DO NOT be too quick to pay it, especially if it is due to fall off your report soon. As I stated numerous times before, negative items stay on your credit report for seven years. The great thing about FICO Scores is that the older the debt, the less impact it has on your score TODAY. Remember, under the FCRA, negative collection accounts can ONLY stay on your credit report for seven years from when you stopped paying on the account, which is the date of the first delinquency.

Before, if you paid off an old collection account, it would renew the date of the recent activity and would actually create a negative impact on your credit score by staying on your report for another seven years from the date you made the payment. But with the recent enhancements made by FICO, paying off old debt or leaving it, does not hurt your score because the FICO system now knows which are old delinquencies and which are new ones. (There are lesser penalties for those that are old).

The only time I would suggest paying off old debt that is due to fall off soon (two and a half years or less) is if you are in the process of obtaining new credit. Lenders do not ONLY look at your FICO Score when making lending decisions, they look at other factors that say whether or not you are creditworthy. Your payment patterns are important and lenders judge you based on your commitment to meet your financial obligations. Many of them view paying off old debt as a sign of goodwill and an indication that you have changed your ways. Lenders love to see that even if you had some hiccups along the way, you are responsible enough to pay what you owe.

# Step 6 – Snowball Your Debt

Now that you have a grip on the negative and past due items that were affecting your credit, it's time to pay down your debt in order to bring down your usage ratio. As a quick refresher, your usage ratio is the amount of money you owe compared to the amount available to you. For example, if you have a credit card with a $1,000 credit limit and use $500, your debt usage ratio is 50%. As you can recall from the FICO Score breakdown, debt utilization is 30% of your score, making it the second most important factor to take control of when trying to repair your credit or maintain a good credit history. As a rule of thumb your usage ratio should be between 20% and 30%. The lower your ratio is, the better it looks to the credit bureaus. The simplest way to change your ratio is by paying down your balances and NOT closing accounts.

Most people concentrating on paying down debt think about the most logical step, which is to pay down the debt that has the highest interest rate. But snowballing debt is actually the opposite. Many financial advisors cringe at this, but I (including some other reputable folks) say FORGET the interest rate! Managing debt and your finances is just as psychological as it is practical. The concept of snowballing debt is simply paying down your smallest debt first then using the money from the paid off debt to tackle the next smallest. Doing this gives you some small victories early on, which helps build the perception that you are making progress. No matter what the interest rates are, if you have ten credit accounts and you are able to pay off three of them in a matter of months, it gives you the confidence and motivation you need in order to succeed.

### Steps to snowballing debt:
1) Using the sheet on the next page—make copies or download at www. WhatTheFico.com/SnowBall—list all of your debts in order, from the smallest to the largest. Again, FORGET about the interest rate! (The only time you should be concerned with the rate is if two debts have the same or similar payoff balances. In that instance pay off the debt with the highest rate).

# What the FICO!

2) Pay the minimum payment on all of your debts except for the smallest one. With what you have left over, pay down the smallest as much as you can and as fast as you can. Every time you get any extra money, you need to keep paying the smallest debt until it disappears.

3) Every time a debt is paid off, add whatever you were paying as its minimum payment to your next debt payment, plus any extra amount available.

4) Redo the sheet every time you pay off a debt so that you can see how close you are to being debt free! Make sure you keep the old sheets as a reminder too!

# 12 Steps to Repairing Your Credit

## Debt Snowball

| Item | Total Payoff | Minimum Payment | New Payment |
|------|--------------|-----------------|-------------|
|  |  |  |  |
|  |  |  |  |
|  |  |  |  |
|  |  |  |  |
|  |  |  |  |
|  |  |  |  |
|  |  |  |  |
|  |  |  |  |
|  |  |  |  |
|  |  |  |  |
|  |  |  |  |
|  |  |  |  |
|  |  |  |  |
|  |  |  |  |
|  |  |  |  |
|  |  |  |  |
|  |  |  |  |
|  |  |  |  |
|  |  |  |  |
|  |  |  |  |
|  |  |  |  |
|  |  |  |  |
|  |  |  |  |
|  |  |  |  |

# Step 7 – Keep Some Credit Accounts Open (But Cut up the Cards)

Now that you have begun to eliminate your debt, you don't want to find yourself back in the same rut by being tempted with all of that available credit you now have. To remove the temptation you have two options: close the accounts or cut up the cards. In order to have a healthy credit file, you should at least have five tradelines open and in good standing. I also suggest that you have at least one or two credit cards opened for emergency purposes. When closing accounts, make sure you ONLY close one or two accounts every six months or so. Creditors view a sudden burst of activity of any kind as red flag that there may be some issues with your financial stability. When deciding which accounts to keep open or which to close, keep at least the one or two oldest accounts so that you can take advantage of the credit history. (Remember, the third biggest factor in your credit score is length of credit history).

**Steps on how to decide whether to keep or close accounts:**
1) Take a look at your credit report and identify all revolving credit accounts (This includes all credit cards, home equity lines of credits, and any other account that allows you to use the funds as you pay it back).
2) Add up all of your credit limits and add up all of your outstanding balances.
3) Divide your outstanding balances by your credit limits and use that number to determine your usage ratio.
4a) If your ratio is between 20 and 30%, then leave all accounts open and continue to pay down debt.
4b) If your ratio is lower (0%-@20%) list your accounts in order by opening date. Recalculate your ratio by removing the newest account to see if you still fall between 20% and 30% or lower. If you do, then it's OK to close that account.
5) Determine which one or two cards you are going to use for emergency purposes, then cut up the rest. Take those one or two cards and put them in a bowl. Fill that bowl up with water then put it in the freezer. I know what you're thinking, but I am dead serious! This will eliminate any temptations. In case of an emergency, break the glass or heat the ice.

# Step 8 – Get a Secured Credit Card

With payment history being 35% of your credit score, it is impossible to rebuild good credit without reestablishing a positive payment history. Your creditors want to know that you are creditworthy, but with your past credit issues still looming over your head, creditors are going to be reluctant to extend new credit without seeing that you have adopted new habits…talk about a catch-22! Well, have no fear! A secured credit card can help you reestablish yourself and begin you toward financial freedom.

It is a fact that adding good tradelines to your credit profiles WILL increase your credit score. That's what makes a secured credit card such a powerful tool. As an example, if you were to add one good credit account to your profile and have just one bad credit account deleted, your score could increase by as much as 80 points with just those two actions.

So how does a secured credit card work? Simply, the bank that issues you the credit card requires you to deposit money into a savings account or CD (Certificate of Deposit). That money will be put on hold and used as collateral in case you default and cannot pay it back. Your deposit will earn interest and be kept in its respective account until the lender decides that you are creditworthy enough for an unsecured card. It usually takes between one year and 18 months for the lender to give you an unsecured card, but it's based on your repayment history. Specifically, how well you paid back your bills on time and if you kept your usage ratio below 30%. In the event that they determine you are creditworthy, they will send you back your deposit plus interest, and give you a credit card based solely on your creditworthiness and no collateral.

All secured credit cards are not created equally. Below are the steps needed to decide which will work best for you:

## 1) Find out who offers a secured credit card.
Check Bankrate.com's list of secured credit card issuers to get a good idea of who offers what. If you belong to a credit union, As you should, ask them about their secured loan products. Most credit unions do offer them and may give you a lower interest rate and/or waive any annual fees.

**2) Compare the different cards to determine what kind of charges will be assessed.**

All secured cards charge an annual fee but look for one that doesn't charge an application fee. Make sure that you READ the fine print! Secured cards are designed for those with bad or no credit, so some unscrupulous lenders have taken advantage of this by killing you with fees that are hidden in the fine print. As you compare, look for those with the lowest interest rates and fees.

**3) Make sure you choose a lender who reports to all three major credit bureaus.**

Let's be clear, the ONLY reason you want or need a secured credit card is to rebuild your credit. If the lender you choose does not report to all three credit bureaus, then you are defeating the purpose. In making a decision as to which lender you are going to apply with, make sure you ask whether they report to the Big Three. Also, find out if the card issuer will flag your card and report to the credit bureaus that it is a secured card. If they do, look for an issuer that doesn't. The fact that you have a secured card should just be between you and the lender. Most good secured cards report it as a regular credit card and use the deposit as assurance of repayment. (Having a flag on your report that identifies your card as a secured card can hurt your credit rather than help it.)

**4) Figure out how much you can afford to deposit and choose a card.**

Now that you have identified a lender, figure out how much you can afford to deposit. The amount you can deposit will vary by issuer, but most start as low as $250 and go as high as $5,000. Your credit limit will either be the amount of your deposit or some percentage above that amount. (Keep in mind that once you make an initial deposit you CANNOT add more money later.)

**5) Make the best use of your secured card to build your credit rating.**

Your main objective in getting a secured card is to show creditors that you can pay your bills on time. DO NOT use the card if you CANNOT pay your bill in full every month! Buy a few things then pay it off. Make sure that you are staying between 20% and 30% of your credit limit in order to keep your usage ratio in good standing. For example if you have a $1,000 credit limit, pretend as if your limit is ONLY $300 and NEVER spend more than that amount.

Congratulations! You are on your way to debt and financial freedom! Remember, secured credit cards are a tool to rebuild credit. Once you have reestablished yourself in the credit world, it is important that you get a credit card that doesn't charge an annual fee.

# Step 9 – Join a Credit Union

I get asked many times, "Which is better, a credit union or a traditional bank?" Honestly, there really isn't a "better" because it's all a matter of preference and need. But when it comes to repairing your credit and rebuilding your financial future, a credit union should be a part of the equation.

During the great recession of 2008, there were many battles: Wall Street vs. Main Street, Big Bank vs. Small Bank, the credit crunch, too big to fail, the move your money movement, Occupy Wall Street, and many more. Throughout these battles the one thing that could not be denied is that every financial institution serves its own unique purpose.

So what's the difference between a credit union and a traditional bank? The main differences between the two are ownership and objective. A traditional bank is a for-profit business owned by its investors and shareholders with its main objective of increasing shareholders' profits. A credit union is a not-for-profit organization owned by its members (depositors) with its main objective to serve its members.

That's not to say that traditional banks do not serve their customers. In fact, because of vast resources, a traditional bank may be able to do so better. But, above all, a traditional bank exists to make a profit. In fact, a traditional bank is run by a paid board of directors making all of the decisions for the bank, which are usually profit-driven.

Credit unions, on the other hand, are designed to serve a particular group or neighborhood and, again, since they are a not-for-profit organization, the money that they make—after paying overhead costs—directly benefits the members. In a credit union, the members have more say in how the institution is run, and they hold decision-making powers that allow them to elect the board of directors who work for its members.

With that being said, after you recover from your credit issues, make sure you join a credit union. A credit union is more likely to give you loans in the future than a regular bank will. Because of their profit structure, credit unions usually provide lower interest rates on loans and lower-cost services. The more people who deposit money into a credit union, the higher the benefits to the existing members. Another plus is that credit unions are tax-exempt, so that's another set of funds that can be used to its members' benefit.

> **NOTE** Despite the many benefits of a credit union, often banks do offer a wider range of services and are more accessible to customers. My suggestion would be to maintain a savings account at a credit union, which usually pays higher interest rates on savings accounts, while leaving your checking account in a traditional bank.

### Steps to finding a Credit Union to Join:

1) If you work a 9-to-5 job or are connected somehow to an organization, ask if it is affiliated with any credit unions. If it is not, ask about any trade association credit unions you may be eligible for.

2) Find out if your church or house of worship has a credit union, if not check for local credit unions within your specific religion.

3) Do a Google or Bing search for credit unions in your area. You can also use a credit union search site, like www.CreditUnionsOnline.com, which will list credit unions you qualify for.

4) Some credit unions allow family members to join. Find out if anyone in your family is a member of one and ask if the institution accepts family member applications.

# Step 10 – Follow the 30 Day Rule

Impulse spending is to budget and debt as fried food and soda is to a diet! If you don't get that analogy, I am simply saying that impulse spending will kill your budget and put you back knee-deep into debt. On the road to repairing your credit and creating financial freedom you must understand that impulse spending is your enemy and counter to any progress you have made thus far.

When I say impulse spending, I mean purchases that are unplanned and made on impulse, either while making the decision to buy another product or service or while being exposed to some type of well-crafted promotional message. You know how this works! Impulse spending is purely emotionally driven and tied to our basic want for instant gratification. When we are checking out at the supermarket, we see the magazines, gum, candy, and chocolate ready for us to purchase. It is calling our name and we can't resist. Or what about that new exclusive product that we see on TV that we must have. Or the sale that is too good to be true and the buy one, get one free deals. Oh yeah, we cant forget about our big ticket items, like cars and home appliances, that are sooo deeply discounted that we would be a fool not to buy.

The truth is that impulse spending is a scientifically studied behavior that the marketing teams of many retail corporations study extensively. They know that the mind responds to specific stimuli that makes you buy emotionally and without thinking. Impulse spending disrupts our normal decision making process and makes our brain react differently. The brain's logical function is momentarily put on hold and replaced with an irrational moment of self-gratification.

When you buy an impulse item, you are buying what appeals to your emotional side. Most of these items are never bought out of necessity but, one way or the other, the mind is convinced that it needs this item. Again, this behavior will set you back and prevent you from ever becoming financially free. The best way to avoid impulse spending is to set budgets before you go shopping, as well as taking some time before you make any purchasing decisions. This brings us to the 30-day rule, which is a simple method for controlling impulse spending.

# Steps to following the 30-day rule:

1. The next time your emotions take over and you feel the urge to splurge, take a deep breath. Remind yourself about your goals and force yourself to stop. Even if you are at the checkout with your items…STOP and leave the store!

2. As soon as you get home, take out a piece of paper and write down the date, the name of the item, where you found it, and the how much it cost.

3. Post this piece of paper where you will see it often—like on your calendar, fridge, mirror, or mobile device—as a daily reminder.

4. For the next 30 days, figure out whether you really need (or want) this item, but DO NOT buy it.

5. If, at the end of the month, you still want it, then buy it if you can afford it. (Under NO circumstances can you use credit to buy this item.)

Yup!, that's it! It may not seem like much, but you'll be surprised at how effective this technique is. The great thing about this strategy is that you are not denying yourself anything, you are just delaying gratification. This gives you a real opportunity to really decide from a logical standpoint whether you can really afford this item, do you really even want it, and allows you to do so in a way that doesn't kill your budget or puts you back into debt. It also gives you an opportunity to research this item just in case you can find it somewhere else at a cheaper price.

# Step 11 – Automate Your Savings, Bills, and Spending

Albert Einstein once said, "We cannot solve our problems with the same thinking we used when we created them." This also goes for our actions! You know the saying, "If you keep doing what you've always done, you'll keep getting what you've always gotten." Now that you are on the journey toward financial freedom, automating your finances is the next step needed to ensure success and eliminate any relapse of irresponsible money management. You have trusted yourself before and see where it got you? In debt! And now that you are rebuilding a more solid structure, you do not want to chance the possibility of going back. The automation of finances was first introduced to me while reading David Bach's bestselling book *The Automatic Millionaire*. He gives tips on how to "get rich slowly" and explains the importance of paying yourself first. We will now take this concept a step further by introducing the automation of your savings, bills, and spending. This method is effective because once you set it up, the only thing you have to do is spend money! Yup!, that's it. Spend, spend, spend! (I knew you would like the sound of that.)

**Here's how it works:**
1) From the budget you created in step three, figure out how much money needs to go to savings, bills, and spending. My wife and I use what's called 10/10/10. That's where 10% of all of our income goes to savings, 10% goes to spending, and 10% goes to giving, which we'll talk about in step 12. The rest goes to bills and anything left over goes to paying down debt. You can use this model as a guide or come up with the percentages that work best for your situation. But it is IMPERATIVE that you save, spend, and give a percentage of your income. Also note that when I say spend, I mean spend on anything you want…no restrictions. (This assures that you don't feel deprived and lessens the risk of you veering off of your budget.)

2) Make sure you have three accounts; a savings account and two checking. Your savings account should be at a credit union or an

Internet bank like CapitalOne360, formerly **Ing Direct**. (Having your savings account in a less accessible financial institution helps curve the temptation of using the funds for anything other than saving and emergencies.) One checking account should be for bills and the other for spending. The account that is designated for bills SHOULD NOT have a debit card associated with it. Having a debit card makes your bill account too accessible.

3) Once you have those set up, have your funds directly deposited into each account respectively. If your employer does not allow for split deposits then have everything go into the bill account (since you don't have a debit card for that account) then automatically transfer to the others using recurring transfers via your bank's online banking system.

4) From your bill account, set up recurring payments for as many of your bills as you can, including rent and cable. The remaining bills that cannot be automated because they depend on usage, for example electricity, should be paid via online banking once you receive the bill. Anything that is not a bill but is part of your budget should be paid with cash. You must go into the bank and make a withdrawal ONLY for the amount designated in your budget for these specific items. This includes things like groceries, transportation, haircuts, or the salon. The money that is in your savings account stays there and what is in your spending account is yours to do what you see fit.

5) Review and execute this process monthly. This is in no way a set-it-and-forget-it type of plan. In order to be successful you have to readjust as needed with the ultimate goal being to save more and pay down debt! In the event that you want to spend money on something specific that your 10% spending allocation can't cover, make sure you re-budget your expenses to do so. (Again, you should NOT use credit.)

# Step 12 – Pay It Forward

Now that you understand how FICO works, why it's important to set a budget, and how to automate your finances you are well on your way to reaching ALL of your financial goals. With this new found knowledge, the only thing that can stop you is YOU! The very last step in total financial freedom involves a concept that may be hard to grasp. In recent years, many new thought leaders have begun to write about the concept of the Law of Attraction and many have come to the conclusion that "like attracts like." By focusing on positive or negative thoughts, you bring about positive or negative results. It's sort of like how the elders used to say, "You reap what you sow."Yup!, that's the Law of Attraction! I subscribe to this concept 1,000%! There are many examples that I can give you, but to do so I would need to dedicate a entire book to it. What I need to leave you with though is the concept of "paying it forward." Paying it forward is like the Law of Attraction's twin brother! It's the concept that the more you give the more you get! It's "You reap what you sow" on steroids! The only caveat is that you will ONLY reap rewards from giving when you have no expectation of anything in return, so keep that in mind as you attempt this step. Doing good with the expectation of reward is not actually "doing good," you have to be genuine about it then watch how your life changes.

There's no coincidence that the people who give the most are the ones who have the most!Yes, you may say that they have it to give, but the truth is that the giving came first. It might have not been monetarily, but somehow that person's generosity was returned in abundance. Starting immediately, I need you to get used to giving! Not with an ulterior motive, but with an open heart, to someone who CANNOT repay you. Your purpose in life is to leave the world better than how you found it! Give back what has been given to you, and help push the world forward! You have more power than you use and can help more than you think.

This might be the moment where you ask yourself, "What does this have to do with fixing my credit?"To that I won't give you a direct answer, but I will say that the fact that you are reading this book means that you are ready to take your life to the next level. In order to do so you must be willing to give what you want to receive. Jim Rohn once said "Giving is better than receiving because giving starts the receiving process." This concept is the key to an abundant life! Start today by becoming the best that you can possibly be!

**Steps to Paying it Forward:**
1) Pay attention to the different opportunities you have to help someone. It can be an elderly or disabled neighbor or the homeless person looking for a hot meal. It can be mentoring someone looking to get into your same field or making an anonymous donation to your favorite charity. Whatever it is, there are many opportunities daily to help! We just need to open our eyes to it.
2) Do something nice for someone you don't know (or don't know that well). It should be something significant, and for someone you DON'T expect anything in return.
3) If you do something nice for a person and they are interested in repaying you, make sure you ask them to "pay it forward" instead. Let them know that you'd like them to do something nice for three people they don't know and then ask those three people to do something nice for three more people. The goal is to create an epidemic of people helping people just because.
4) When someone does something nice for you, make sure you make a mental note of this in your mind and then do something nice for three other people, as described in the previous step.

**NOTE** Never stop someone from doing something nice for you, by doing so you are blocking their blessing and hindering them from living an abundant life!

# Knowledge Re-Test

What is a credit score?

_____

_____

What are credit ratings?

_____

_____

What are your current credit scores?

_____

_____

_____

Who are the three credit score providers

_____

_____

_____

What factors influence your credit score?

_____

_____

_____

**How does your credit score affect you?**

_____

_____

_____

**What is a "good" credit score?**

_____

_____

**How do you improve your credit score?**

_____

_____

_____

# NOTES

## Resources

# The Credit Bureaus (The Big Three)

The main three credit bureaus in the United States are Experian, Equifax and TransUnion (Better known as the Big Three).

### Addresses for Credit Bureaus

**Experian**
P.O. Box 2002
Allen, TX 75013
**Equifax Credit Information Services, Inc.**
P.O. Box 740256
Atlanta, GA 30374
**TransUnion, LLC**
P.O. Box 2000
Chester, PA 19022

# The Credit Bureaus (The Big Three)

## Credit Bureau Contact Phone Numbers
**Experian**
(888) 397-3742
**Equifax**
(800) 685-1111
**TransUnion, LLC**
(800) 888-4213

## Order Your Credit Report

Besides the FREE credit report you are entitled to annually from **www. AnnualCreditReport.com**, you can also get a FREE report if you have been denied credit, employment, or insurance in the last 60 days. Make sure that you order only the credit report.

- **Equifax** 1-800-685-1111 - They will mail it to you within 48 hours.
- **TransUnion** 1-800-888-4213 - receive within 6 to 8 business days.
- **Experian** 1-888-397-3742 - receive within 8 to 10 business days.

# Helpful Websites

**www.AnnualCreditReport.com** - This central site allows you to request a free **credit file disclosure**, commonly called a credit report, once every 12 months from each of the nationwide consumer credit reporting companies: Equifax, Experian and TransUnion.

AnnualCreditReport.com is the official site to help consumers to obtain their free credit report.

**www.MyFico.com** - Get the score that lenders use most, from the company that invented it. MYFICO provides you immediate access to your FICO score and credit report online.

**www.TransUnion.com** - Total credit protection all in one place from credit alerts, credit reports and credit scores. Get your free credit score today from TRANSUNION, The Source!

**www.Equifax.com** - Get your credit report and credit score from EQUIFAX. Monitor your credit and help protect your identity with identity theft protection from EQUIFAX.

**www.Experian.com** - Check your credit report and credit score with toll-free support, business credit reports, identity theft protection, and marketing solutions - EXPERIAN Official Site.

**www.AskAshCash.com** - The official question and answer of Financial expert Ash Cash. If you have any questions you can email Ash Cash at Questions@IamAshCash.com

## The Credit Bureaus (The Big Three)

**National Foundation for Credit Counseling (www.NFCC.org)** - As the nation's largest financial counseling organization, the NFCC Member Agency Network includes more than 700 community-based offices located in all 50 states and Puerto Rico. More than 3 million consumers annually receive financial counseling and education from NFCC Member Agencies in person, over the phone, or online. **To locate an NFCC Member Agency in your area call 800-388-2227. Para ayuda en Español Ilama al 800-682-9832.**

# Glossary of Credit Terms

## A

**Account Condition:** Indicates the present state of the account, but does not indicate the payment history of the account that led to the current state. (i.e. open, paid, charge off, repossession, settled, foreclosed, etc).

**Account number:** The unique number assigned by a creditor to identify your account with them. Some credit bureaus removes several digits of each account number on the credit report as a fraud prevention measure.

**Accounts in Good Standing:** Credit items that have a positive status and should reflect favorably on your creditworthiness.

**Adjustment:** Percentage of the debt that is to be repaid to the credit grantors in a Chapter 13 bankruptcy.

**Annual fee:** Credit card issuers often (but not always) require you to pay a special charge once a year for the use of their service, usually between $15 and $55.

**Annual percentage rate (APR):** A measure of how much interest credit will cost you, expressed as an annual percentage.

# Glossary of Credit Terms

**Authorized User:** Person permitted by a credit cardholder to charge goods and services on the cardholder's account but who is not responsible for repayment of the debt. The account displays on the credit reports of the cardholder as well as the authorized user. If you wish to have your name permanently removed as an authorized user on an account, you will need to notify the credit grantor.

# B

**Balloon Payments:** A loan with a balloon payment requires that a single, lump-sum payment be made at the end of the loan.

**Bankruptcy Code:** Federal laws governing the conditions and procedures under which persons claiming inability to repay their debts can seek relief.

# C

**Capacity:** Factor in determining creditworthiness. Capacity is assessed by weighing a borrower's earning ability and the likelihood of continuing income against the amount of debt the borrower carries at the time the application for credit is made. While capacity may be considered in a credit decision, the credit report does not contain information about earning ability or the likelihood of continuing income.

**Chapter 7 Bankruptcy:** Chapter of the Bankruptcy Code that provides for court administered liquidation of the assets of a financially troubled individual or business.

**Chapter 11 Bankruptcy:** Chapter of the Bankruptcy Code that is usually used for the reorganization of a financially troubled business. Used as an alternative to liquidation under Chapter 7. The U.S. Supreme Court has held that an individual may also use Chapter 11.

**Chapter 12 Bankruptcy:** Chapter of the Bankruptcy Code adopted to address the financial crisis of the nation's farming community. Cases under this chapter are administered like Chapter 11 cases, but with special protections to meet the special conditions of family farm operations.

**Chapter 13 Bankruptcy:** Chapter of the Bankruptcy Code in which debtors repay debts according to a plan accepted by the debtor, the creditors and the court. Plan payments usually come from the debtor's future income and are paid to creditors through the court system and the bankruptcy trustee.

**Charge-Off:** Action of transferring accounts deemed uncollectible to a category such as bad debt or loss. Collectors will usually continue to solicit payments, but the accounts are no longer considered part of a company's receivable or profit picture.

**Civil Action:** Any court action against a consumer to regain money for someone else. Usually, it will be a wage assignment, child support judgment, small claims judgment or a civil judgment.

**Claim Amount:** The amount awarded in a court action.

**Closed Date:** The date an account was closed.

**Co-maker:** A creditworthy co-maker is sometimes required in situations where an applicant's qualifications are marginal. A co-maker is legally responsible to repay the charges in the joint account agreement.
**Consumer Credit Counseling Service:** A non-profit organization that assists consumers in dealing with their credit problems. Consumer Credit Counseling Service has offices throughout the United States that can be located by calling 800 388 CCCS (2227).

**Co-signer:** Person who pledges in writing as part of a credit contract to repay the debt if the borrower fails to do so. The account displays on both the borrower's and the co-signer's credit reports.

# Glossary of Credit Terms

**Credit Limit/Line of Credit:** In open-end credit, the maximum amount a borrower can draw upon or the maximum that an account can show as outstanding.

**Credit Items:** Information reported by current or past creditors.

**Credit Report:** Confidential report on a consumer's payment habits as reported by their creditors to a consumer credit reporting agency. The agency provides the information to credit grantors who have a permissible purpose under the law to review the report.

**Credit Scoring:** Tool used by credit grantors to provide an objective means of determining risks in granting credit. Credit scoring increases efficiency and timely response in the credit granting process. Credit scoring criteria is set by the credit grantor.

**Creditworthiness:** The ability of a consumer to receive favorable consideration and approval for the use of credit from an establishment to which they applied.

# D

**Date Filed:** The date that a public record was awarded.

**Date of Status:** On the credit report, date the creditor last reported information about the account.

**Date Opened:** On the credit report, indicates the date an account was opened.

**Date Resolved:** The completion date or satisfaction date of a public record item.

**Delinquent:** Accounts classified into categories according to the time past due. Common classifications are 30, 60, 90 and 120 days past due. Special classifications also include charge-off, repossession, transferred, etc.

**Discharge:** Granted by the court to release a debtor from most of his debts that were included in a bankruptcy. Any debts not included in the bankruptcy – alimony, child support, liability for willful and malicious conduct and certain student loans – cannot be discharged.

**Disclosure:** Providing the consumer with his or her credit history as required by the FCRA. Credit bureaus provide consumer credit report disclosures via the Internet, by U.S. Mail or sometimes in person.

**Dismissed:** When a consumer files a bankruptcy, the judge may decide to not allow the consumer to continue with the bankruptcy. If the judge rules against the petition, the bankruptcy is known as dismissed.

**Dispute:** If a consumer believes an item of information on their credit report is inaccurate or incomplete, they may challenge, or dispute the item. Credit bureaus will investigate and correct or remove any inaccurate information or information that cannot be verified. Credit bureaus give consumers the option of disputing online or they may call the telephone number on their credit report for assistance.

# E

**ECOA:** Standard abbreviation for Equal Credit Opportunity Act.

**End-user:** The business that receives the report for decision making purposes that meet the permissible purpose requirements of the FCRA.

**Equal Credit Opportunity Act (ECOA):** Federal law, which prohibits creditors from discriminating against credit applicants on the basis of sex, marital status, race, color, religion, age, and/or receipt of public assistance.

# Glossary of Credit Terms

**Equifax:** One of the three national credit reporting agencies, headquartered in Atlanta, Ga. The other two are Experian and TransUnion.

**Experian:** One of the three national credit reporting agencies, with U.S. headquarters in Costa Mesa, CA. The other two are Equifax and TransUnion.

# F

**Fair Credit and Charge Card Disclosure Act:** Amendments to the Truth In Lending Act that require the disclosure of the costs involved in credit card plans that are offered by mail, telephone or applications distributed to the general public.

**Fair Credit Billing Act:** Federal legislation that provides a specific error resolution procedure to protect credit card customers from making payments on inaccurate billings.

**Fair Credit Reporting Act (FCRA):** Federal legislation governing the actions of credit reporting agencies.

**Fair Debt Collection Practices Act (FDCPA):** Federal legislation prohibiting abusive and unfair debt collection practices.

**Finance Charge:** Amount of interest. Finance charges are usually included in the monthly payment total.

**Fixed Rate:** An annual percentage rate that does not change.

# G

**Geographical Code:** This information is received from the Census Bureau and represents the state, Metropolitan Statistical Area, county, tract and block group of the reported address. This code is similar to a ZIP CodeTM.

**Grace Period:** The time period you have to pay a bill in full and avoid interest charges.

**Guarantor:** Person responsible for paying a bill.

# H

**High Balance:** The highest amount that you have owed on an account to date.

# I

**Installment Credit:** Credit accounts in which the debt is divided into amounts to be paid successively at specified intervals.

**Investigation:** The process a consumer credit reporting agency goes through in order to verify credit report information disputed by a consumer. The credit grantor who supplied the information is contacted and asked to review the information and report back; they will tell the credit reporting agency that the information is accurate as it appears, or they will give them corrected information to update the report.

**Investigative Consumer Reports:** These are consumer reports that are usually done for background checks, security clearances and other sensitive jobs. An investigative consumer report might contain information obtained from a credit report, but it is more comprehensive than a credit report. It contains subjective material on an individual's character, habits and mode of living, which is obtained through interviews of associates. Credit bureaus do not provide investigative consumer reports.

**Involuntary Bankruptcy:** A petition filed by certain credit grantors to have a debtor judged bankrupt. If the bankruptcy is granted, it is known as an involuntary bankruptcy.

# Glossary of Credit Terms

**Item-specific Statement:** Offers an explanation about a particular trade or public record item on your report, and it displays with that item on the credit report.

## J

**Judgment Granted:** The determination of a court upon matters submitted to it. A final determination of the rights of the parties involved in the lawsuit.

## L

**Last Reported:** On the credit report, the date the creditor last reported information about the account.

**Liability amount:** Amount for which you are legally obligated to a creditor.

**Lien:** Legal document used to create a security interest in another's property. A lien is often given as a security for the payment of a debt. A lien can be placed against a consumer for failure to pay the city, county, state or federal government money that is owed. It means that the consumer's property is being used as collateral during repayment of the money that is owed.

**Line of Credit:** In open-end credit, the maximum amount a borrower can draw upon or the maximum that an account can show as outstanding.
**Location Number:** The book and page number on which the item is filed in the court records.

## M

**Mortgage Identification Number (MIN):** Indicates that a loan is registered with Mortgage Electronic Registration Systems Inc., which tracks the ownership of mortgage rights. This number will follow the homeowner throughout the mortgage.

**Most Recent Date:** The date of the recent account condition or payment status. This date is also the balance date.

# N

**Notice of Results:** If your investigation results in information being updated or deleted, you may request that we send the corrected information in your credit history to eligible credit grantors and employers who reviewed your information within a specific period of time. If your investigation does not result in a change to your credit history, results will not be sent to other lenders.

# O

**Obsolescence:** A term used to describe how long negative information should stay in a credit file before it's not relevant to the credit granting decision. The FCRA has determined the obsolescence period to be 10 years in the case of bankruptcy and 7 years in all other instances. Unpaid tax liens may remain indefinitely, although some credit bureaus removes them after a certain period of time determined by the bureau.

**Opt In:** The ability of a consumer who has opted out to have their name re-added to prescreened credit and insurance offer lists, direct marketing lists and individual reference service lists. Consumers who have previously opted out of receiving prescreened offers may have their names added to prescreened lists for credit and insurance offers by calling 1 888 5OPTOUT (1 888 567 8688).

**Opt Out:** The ability of the consumer to notify credit reporting agencies, direct marketers and list compilers to remove their name from all future lists. Consumers may opt out of prescreened credit and insurance offer lists by calling 1 888 5OPTOUT (1 888 567 8688).

**Original Amount:** The original amount owed to a creditor.


# P

**Payment Status:** Reflects the previous history of the account, including any delinquencies or derogatory conditions occurring during the previous seven years (i.e., Current account, delinquent 30, current was 60, redeemed repossession, charge-off – now paying, etc.)

**Permissible Purposes:** There are legally defined permissible purposes for a credit report to be issued to a third party. Permissible purposes include credit transactions, employment purposes, insurance underwriting, government financial responsibility laws, court orders, subpoenas, written instructions of the consumer, legitimate business needs, etc.

**Personal Information:** Information on your personal credit report associated with your records that has been reported to us by you, your creditors and other sources. It may include name variations, your driver's license number, Social Security number variations, your date or year of birth, your spouse's name, your employers, your telephone numbers, and information about your residence.

**Personal Statement:** You may request that a general explanation about the information on your report be added to your report. The statement remains for two years and displays to anyone who reviews your credit information.

**Petition:** If a consumer files a bankruptcy, but a judge has not yet ruled that it can proceed, it is known as bankruptcy petitioned.

**Plaintiff:** One who initially brings legal action against another (defendant) seeking a court decision.

**Potentially Negative Items:** Any potentially negative credit items or public records that may have an effect on your creditworthiness as viewed by creditors.

**Public Record Data:** Included as part of the credit report, this information is limited to tax liens, lawsuits and judgments that relate to the consumer's debt obligations.

# R

**Recent Balance:** The most recent balance owed on an account as reported by the creditor.

**Recent Payment:** The most recent amount paid on an account as reported by the creditor.

**Released:** This means that a lien has been satisfied in full.

**Report Number:** A number that uniquely identifies each personal credit report. This number displays on your personal credit report and should always be referenced when you contact the credit buruea.

**Reported Since:** On the credit report, the date the creditor started reporting the account to the credit buruea.

**Repossession:** A creditor's taking possession of property pledged as collateral on a loan contract on which a borrower has fallen significantly behind in payments.

**Request an Investigation:** If you believe that information on your report is inaccurate, the credit bureaus will ask the sources of the information to check their records at no cost to you. Incorrect information will be corrected; information that cannot be verified will be deleted. An investigation may take up to 30 days. When it is complete, they'll send you the results.

# Glossary of Credit Terms

**Request for Your Credit History:** When a credit grantor, direct marketer or potential employer makes a request for information from a consumer's credit report, an inquiry is shown on the report. Grantors only see credit inquiries generated by other grantors as a result of an application of some kind, while consumers see all listed inquiries including prescreened and direct marketing offers, as well as employment inquiries. According to the Fair Credit Reporting Act, credit grantors with a permissible purpose may inquire about your credit information prior to your consent. This section also includes the date of the inquiry and how long the inquiry will remain on your report.

**Responsibility:** Indicates who is responsible for an account; can be single, joint, co-signer, etc.

**Revolving Account:** Credit automatically available up to a predetermined maximum limit so long as a customer makes regular payments.

**Risk Scoring Models:** A numerical determination of a consumer's creditworthiness. Tool used by credit grantors to predict future payment behavior of a consumer.

# S

**Satisfied:** If the consumer has paid all of the money the court says he owes, the public record item is satisfied.

**Secured Credit:** Loan for which some form of acceptable collateral, such as a house or automobile has been pledged.

**Security:** Real or personal property that a borrower pledges for the term of a loan. Should the borrower fail to repay, the creditor may take ownership of the property by following legally mandated procedures.

**Security Alert:** Statement that is added once a credit bureau is notified that a consumer may be a victim of fraud. It remains on file for 90 days and requests that a creditor request proof of identification before granting credit in that person's name.

**Service Credit:** Agreements with service providers. You receive goods, such as electricity, and services, such as apartment rental and health club memberships, with the agreement that you will pay for them each month. Your contract may require payments for a specific number of months, even if you stop the service.

**Settle:** Reach an agreement with a lender to repay only part of the original debt.

**Source:** The business or organization that supplied certain information that appears on the credit report.

**Status:** On the credit report, this indicates the current status or state of the account.

# T

**Terms:** This refers to the debt repayment terms of your agreement with a creditor, such as 60 months, 48 months, etc.

**Third-Party Collectors:** Collectors who are under contract to collect debts for a credit department or credit company; collection agency.

**Tradeline:** Entry by a credit grantor to a consumer's credit history maintained by a credit reporting agency. A tradeline describes the consumer's account status and activity. Tradeline information includes names of companies where the applicant has accounts, dates accounts were opened, credit limits, types of accounts, balances owed and payment histories.

# Glossary of Credit Terms

**Transaction fees:** Fees charged for certain use of your credit line – for example, to get a cash advance from an ATM.

**TransUnion:** One of three national credit reporting agencies. The other two are Experian and Equifax.

**Truth in Lending Act:** Title I of the Consumer Protection Act. Requires that most categories of lenders disclose the annual interest rate, the total dollar cost and other terms of loans and credit sales.

**Type:** This refers to the type of credit agreement made with a creditor; for example, a revolving account or installment loan.

# U

**Unsecured Credit:** Credit for which no collateral has been pledged. Loans made under this arrangement are sometimes called signature loans; in other words, a loan is granted based only on the customer's words, through signing an agreement that the loan amount will be paid.

# V

**Vacated:** Indicates a judgment that was rendered void or set aside.

**Variable Rate:** An annual percentage rate that may change over time as the prime lending rate varies or according to your contract with the lender.

**Verification:** Verifying whether data in a credit report is correct or not. Initiated by consumers when they question some information in their file. Credit reporting agencies will accept authentic documentation from the consumer that will help in the verification.

# What the FICO!

**Victim Statement:** A statement that can be added to a consumer's credit report to alert credit grantors that a consumer's identification has been used fraudulently to obtain credit. The statement requests the credit grantor to contact the consumer by telephone before issuing credit. It remains on file for 7 years unless the consumer requests that it be removed.

**Voluntary Bankruptcy:** If a consumer files the bankruptcy on his own, it is known as voluntary bankruptcy.

# W

**Wage assignment:** A signed agreement by a buyer or borrower, permitting a creditor to collect a certain portion of the debtor's wages from an employer in the event of default.

**Withdrawn:** This means a decision was made not to pursue a bankruptcy, a lien, etc. after court documents have been filed.

**Writ of Replevin:** Legal document issued by a court authorizing repossession of security.

# ABOUT THE AUTHOR

Ash Exantus a.k.a. ASH CASH is a motivational speaker, business consultant, financial literacy educator, and the author of Amazon. com bestselling book, Mind Right, Money Right: 10 Laws of Financial

Freedom, as well as Taylor's Way: Life Lesson Through The Eyes of a Three Year Old. Ash Cash travels the world helping everyday people get their lives back in order, whether they need financial advice or a little motivation via his special way of conveying life lessons. As a banking professional for more than 10 years, he has led and managed branches for some of the largest financial institutions in the world, controlling

# ABOUT THE AUTHOR

over $400 million dollars in deposits throughout his career. During his service as a banking executive, Ash Cash has helped countless people to recover their financial lives – from credit, to homeownership, retirement, and banking and investments. And, as a Certified FICO Professional (FICO PRO, a national designation), Ash Cash has a strong understanding of FICO® scores and how they impact both the lender and consumer.

Others may know Ash Cash from his Motivational Column titled "The Daily Word", which reaches thousands of people daily through his own e-mail communiqué, as well as partnerships with high traffic, international websites such as AllHipHop.com and Global14.com, among others. His audio version of "The Daily Word" has garnered over 60,000 listens and is frequently heard in over 39 countries. Ash Cash also lends his expertise as a Personal Finance Expert and Contributing Writer for AllHipHop.com, RadioOne, The Huffington Post/Black Voices, and MSNBC affiliate website, TheGrio.com. He has been featured on popular, national media outlets such as Hot97FM and WBLS 107.5FM in New York City, nationally syndicated Café Mocha Radio, CNN, Black Enterprise Magazine, Essence Magazine, Rolling Out, The Atlanta Post, and countless others.

Ash Cash is the proud Founder of T.E.A.M. F.R.E.S.H. (Taking Every Amicable Measure to Financially Reeducate Every Spectrum of Humanity), a program that works with schools, correctional facilities, churches, and community-based organizations, to teach Financial Literacy and Entrepreneurship skills to at risk youth in urban settings. He also serves on the Board of Directors for Egypt Cares Family Foundation, a non-profit organization founded by TV Host and Radio Personality, Egypt Sherrod. In addition, he is treasurer and board member for Harlem Cares Mentoring Movement, an affiliate of National Cares Mentoring Movement started by Susan Taylor, former editor-in-chief of Essence Magazine, and also an advisory board member for several nonprofit organizations throughout the country.

## What the FICO!

Above all of his credentials, accolades, and titles, Ash Cash is simply known for making people feel better. He thoroughly enjoys his life in the metropolitan New York, where he works as well as resides with his wife and toddler daughter. For more information on Ash Cash's unique methods for teaching Prosperity and Purpose, please visit **www.IamAshCash.com**

# Also Available by Ash Cash

**M**ind Right, Money Right: 10 Laws of Financial Freedom, is a book designed to teach you how to effectively manage your personal finances. It shows you how having the right mental attitude and with laser sharp focus, you can have anything you desire in life. It's an easy to read book that anyone, at any level, can understand. The book's aim is to teach you these 10 proven Laws of Financial Freedom using the stories of wealthy men and women who have used them. This book is especially geared towards anyone who is tired of having a dependency on money and is ready to take some practical steps in order to correct it. Money is power but knowing how to make it work for you is freedom; Mind Right, Money Right will teach you how.

**H**ave you ever spent time observing a child or group of children and how they conduct their young lives? The one thing you will immediately notice is that they live life by their instincts. They are enthusiastic, always eager to learn, curious, brave, and will try almost anything without hesitation. These characteristics and more are all the keys to happiness but unfortunately as we transition from childhood to adulthood we replace these natural instincts with what adults call "reality." As I watched my daughter Taylor grow, I began to realize that she had not been tainted by our ideas of "reality" and as a result was always happy and tended to get everything she wanted out of life effortlessly. Isn't that what we all want of our lives? In the following pages you will read in detail the valuable lessons I've learned from my three year old daughter. Each chapter illustrates through the eyes of a child how you can live a happier life the way it was intended for you to live! Life is abundant! Life is enjoyable! Life is exactly how you imagined it in your wildest dreams! Today is the day that you bring it back to that essence!

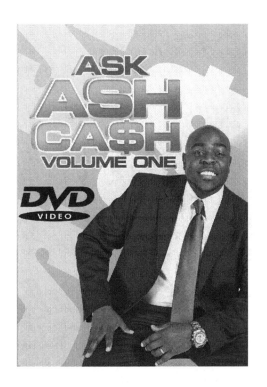

A sk Ash Cash Volume 1 is a DVD series of questions by everyday people wanting to gain financial advice. With more than 14 years of banking under his belt, Ash'Cash is on a mission to financial re-educate every spectrum of humanity

# COMING SOON

**M**ind Right Money Right for Teens, is the newest book in Ash'Cash's bestselling series about how to properly manage and grow your money by having the right thought process. This book doesn't just give you money secrets that will change your life now but the lessons in this book will help change your life forever and give you the financial freedom you deserve. Based on the story of a young millionaire name Ben Frank, this book will show you:

- How to use your confidence to get anything you want in life.

## What the FICO!

- How to get rich by saving and investing your money wisely.

-Why its important to work to learn, not to earn.

-And why giving up is not always a bad thing.

If you are interested in purchasing bulk orders of any of the above books please call 877-853-0493 or write to: 1Brick Publishing C/O Ash Cash Enterprises, LLC - P.O. Box 2717, New York, NY 10027

Made in the USA
Lexington, KY
17 September 2015